AUSTRALIAN COLONIAL FOOD
1850 - 1900

Copyright © 2016 E L Smythe. All rights reserved. No part of this book may be reproduced, stored in a retrieval system, or transmitted in any form or by any means, electronic, mechanical, photocopying, recording, or otherwise, without the prior written permission of the Copyright owner.

ISBN 9780646955742
Proudly self-published 2016

Front cover: Drew, Michael J (1890). *Interior view of family in a kitchen.* State Library of Victoria Picture Collection

Typesetting services by Gunn & Penn
Print on demand services by Ingram Spark
Global distribution services by Ingram Spark

Contents

Introduction	1
About the recipes	3
Meats	5
Poultry	17
Seafood	21
Game	25
Soups & stews	31
Vegetables & accompaniments	41
Sauces	53
Cakes, biscuits & breads	59
Puddings & pancakes	73
Jams, jellies & sherbets	89
Custards & sauces	95
Drinks	99
Around the home	103
Substitutes & modern terms	115
Measures & conversions	119
Index	121

Introduction

Today the Aussie palate is as distinctive as the Aussie accent. It's a giddy mix of international influence that has taken considerable time to find its own identity. From damper to pavlova, our daily menu has been a process of evolution born from necessity, scarcity, and in many respects pure creativity. Before the First Fleet, the Aboriginal population survived as hunter / gatherers, using the best products from the natural environment to develop a distinctive menu of wild meats and fish, accompanied by the natural supermarket of native plants. The early explorers and later immigrant settlers bought with them preserved meats, and food basics such as flour and sugar, as well as seeds and root stock to cultivate crops.

With the gold rush and assisted immigration, Australian fare in the new colony was transformed into a truly international menu. As each nationality sought to bring a little of "the homeland" with them, food quickly became the cornerstone of a multi-cultural stew that was to set Australia on a culinary path so mixed up with the influence of every corner of the world. The British bought the staple roast and sweet sugary puddings, while the Chinese introduced rice, dumplings and sharp salty spices. From southern Europe, coffee, garlic and herbs of all kinds made their way into the dietary offering. Scandinavian and German influences added rich cakes and luxurious soups while the French showed us how to enhance flavours with marinades and sauces. The Irish made use of it all in the omnipresent and often adapted Irish stew as well as new ways to prepare and grow vegetables.

In culinary terms, the period from 1850 to 1900 saw the Australian diet at its most transformative. As each nationality contributed its own to our recipe books, new foods such as kangaroo, wild fish and seemingly exotic fruits gave the new settlers the opportunity to experiment not only with taste but also inventive cooking methods. While some may say the Australian food revolution of the colonial period has only been recently rivalled, what can be found in the history of our food, well before the lamingtons and Vegemite, is the basis for what we know today as typical and everyday Australian fare.

About the recipes

First of all, a caveat. These recipes have not been tested! The instructions given are often not for beginners or feint hearted chefs.

All of the recipes are "of the day". In presentation, they are unlike today's modern form of cookery instructions. There is no list of ingredients. The measures – where they appear - are in the old imperial scale. More so, the recipes are just methods, written in the most basic way. They are imprecise. They are often incomplete. They almost certainly assume a certain level of cooking skill, if not a willingness to adapt and invent.

Reflecting the narrative of the period, the recipes are presented as they were to the cooks of the day with some modern adjustments for ease of reading. Taken from newspapers, books and some from folklore, their reading may be as informative about colonial life in Australia as they are entertaining in their cooking.

Interspersed are various narratives taken from the period providing fascinating insights into the day to day lives of the Australian colonials and their attitudes to food and cookery.

Meats

Beef rump en Matelotte

Cut a beef rump in pieces. Parboil and then stew in broth without seasoning. When about half done stir in a little butter with a spoonful of flour over the fire till brown. Moisten it with a spoonful of the broth then put in the beef. Add half-a-dozen parboiled onions, a glass of sherry, a bunch of parsley, a laurel leaf, a bunch of sweet herbs, pepper and salt. Stew until the rump and onions are done. Skim well and put anchovy and a spoonful of capers (cut small) into the sauce. Boil and serve the rump in the middle of a dish, and the onions round it.

Meat and potato pie

Skin some potatoes and cut them into slices, as well as some mutton, beef, pork, or veal. Season them all and put alternate layers of meat and potatoes in a dish. Bake in oven.

Mutton scallops

Mince dressed mutton with very little fat, season lightly with pepper and salt, and put into a scallop shell, about half full. Then put potatoes mashed with a little milk and a very small bit of butter. Smooth with a spoon and brown in the oven.

Pilau

Boil rice and line a pie dish with ham or lean bacon, sliced very thinly. Cut up a fowl in joints, or part of a breast of veal in pieces. Season with pepper and salt and put to the ham with two large onions stuck with cloves. Then fill up the dish with the rice, lay a common paste (pastry) over. Put a quarter of a pint of gravy in and bake for one hour in a quick oven. Take off the crust before serving, and garnish with hard eggs, boiled onions, and Indian pickle.

Steak or kidney pudding

If kidney, split and soak it, and season that or the meat. Make a pastry of suet, flour and milk. Roll and line a basin with it. Put the kidney or steaks in, cover with pastry and pinch round the edge. Cover with a cloth and boil a considerable time.

Lamb cutlets with spinach

Cut the steaks from the loin and fry them. The spinach is to be stewed and put into the dish first, and then the cutlets round it.

Beef steaks and oyster sauce

Strain off the liquor from the oysters, and throw them into cold water to take off the grit. Simmer the liquor with a bit of mace and lemon peel, then put the oysters in. Stew them a few minutes, add a little cream if you have it, and some butter rubbed in a bit of flour. Let them boil up once and have rump steaks, well-seasoned and broiled, ready for throwing the oyster sauce over the moment you are to serve.

Beefsteak and oyster pie

Take beef steaks that have been well hung and beat them gently with a circular steak beater or rolling pin. Season with pepper, salt, and a little shallot, minced very fine. Fill your dish with alternate layers of steak and oysters. Stew the liquor and beards of the latter with a bit of lemon peel, mace, and a sprig of parsley. When the pie is baked, boil with the above three spoonfuls of cream, and one ounce of butter rubbed in flour. Strain it and put it in the dish.

Minced collops

Mince a fleshy piece of beef (free from skin and gristle) very fine and season with salt and pepper. Mix a good piece of butter in a saucepan, with some flour. When this is well browned put the minced meat to it, and beat it well with a wooden spoon or chopper to keep the collops from getting into lumps. When well browned, add as much boiled water as will make it the proper thickness and let it stew till done. If liked, an onion may be added. Venison and veal collops are made as above. Mince collops will keep some time well packed in a jar and covered like potted meats.

1857

"We observe the most earnest appeals in the form of newspaper advertisements to this country to send out women who can cook, and indeed the health, morals, and civilisation of our colonies, and of our countrymen settled in the western World, seem to depend more on the training of our girls to household duties than thoughtless people would readily believe."

Boiling a ham

If your ham is a poor one you can't manufacture it by cooking into a good one. You can improve it but nothing more. As to cooking, the ham ought to be a year old. It should be soaked one night in cold water. It must then be put in a large pot of cold water and simmered for half an hour. Then pour out the water and put in fresh cold water, and let it simmer (not boil) for twenty-five minutes for every pound in weight. Take it out. Remove the skin, grate bread crumbs over it, and set it in the oven for half an hour, and serve hot. The size of a ham for boiling should range from eight to twelve pounds. In carving a ham there is about as much art as cooking it. Let it be chipped as you would dried beef, the slices being as thin as a shaving. This is done by drawing the carving knife backward quickly. When both boiled and carved as it ought to be, there is no human provender more appetising and very little equally so.

Meat patties

Two ounces of ham, four of chicken or veal, one egg boiled hard. Make a fine powder with three cloves, a blade of mace, pepper and salt. Just before you serve, warm the above with four spoonfuls of rich gravy, the same of cream and an ounce of butter.

China chils

Mince a pint basin of undressed neck of mutton or leg, and some of the fat. Put two onions, a lettuce, a pint of green peas, a teaspoonful of salt, a teaspoonful of pepper, four spoonfuls of water and two or three ounces of clarified butter into a stew pan, closely covered. Simmer for two hours and serve in the middle of a dish of boiled dry rice. If cayenne is approved, add a little.

Marrow bones

To prepare, boil and serve with very hot toast. If too long to serve them undivided, saw them in two, cover the open end with cloth thickly floured and tied close.

Cold beef pudding

Take a piece of tender steak, a bit of ham, and some breast of veal, the beef amounting to three quarters of the whole. Mince the whole as small as possible, cut a piece of good salt pork into the hash, seasoning at the same time. Add salt, pepper, and spice, parsley, garlic, mushrooms, and leeks, bay-leaf and thyme, and half a small wine-glass of brandy. Line an earthen covered dish with slices of pork and fill it with the mince, cover with more slices of pork, and set the lid on, cementing the joints with a paste of flour and vinegar. Place in the oven, bake slowly and cool overnight. To be eaten completely cold.

Staffordshire beef steaks

Beat them a little with a rolling pin. Flour and season, then fry with sliced onion till a fine light brown. Lay the steaks into a stew pan and pour over as much boiling water as will serve for sauce. Stew them very gently for half an hour, and add a spoonful of ketchup and a walnut liquor before you serve.

Chartreuse

Line a copper mould with fat bacon. Lay sliced carrots, and turnips round the edges, then cover with a forcemeat, and put in a fricassee of veal or fowl. Cover the top of the mould with pastry and bake it an hour. Serve it turned out upon a dish.

Sheep's kidneys

For a small dish, procure cure six fresh ones. Take off the thin skin which covers them, and cut them into slices. Put in a stew pan one ounce of butter. When melted and nearly brown, add the kidney with half a teaspoonful of salt, a quarter teaspoon of pepper and half a tablespoon of flour. Mix well together. Add half a wineglass of sherry and a gill of broth. Simmer for a few minutes, and serve very hot. A few raw sliced mushrooms added, are excellent. The kidneys can also be cut in halves, and cooked the same, and dished in a crown on a thin border of mashed potatoes.

Roast pork leg

Choose a small leg of fine young pork. Cut a slit in the knuckle with a sharp knife, and fill the space with sage and onions chopped, and a little pepper and salt. Bake in oven. When half-done, serve the skin in slices, but do not cut deeper than the outer rind. Apple sauce should be served with it.

Meat cakes

Take any cold game, poultry, or meat, and, to give it a little richness, add a little fat bacon or ham, and an anchovy. Mince it fine, season with pepper and salt to liking. Mix thoroughly, and make into small cakes, with bread crumbs, yolks of boiled eggs, onions, sweet herbs, curry powder, or any of the forcemeats. Fry the cakes a light brown, and serve them with good gravy; or put the mixture into a mould, and boil or bake it.

Scotch hotch potch

Cut the breast and backward ribs of mutton in small pieces, as well as two pounds of beef. Simmer covered in water. Two hours before serving add several carrots, turnips, onions, lettuces, peas, and cauliflower or cabbage.

Italian beef steaks

Cut a fine large steak from a rump that has been well hung, or it will do from any tender part. Beat it, season with pepper, salt, and onion. Lay it on an iron stew pan that has a cover to fit quite close, and set it by the side of the fire without any water. Take care it does not burn, but it must have a strong heat. In two or three hours it will be quite tender, and then serve with its own gravy.

Indian burdman stew

Cut up in slices ready-dressed lamb or veal, or a fowl in joints. Put it into a stew pan with two spoonfuls of anchovy essence, three spoonfuls of white wine, an ounce of butter rubbed in flour, an onion sliced thin, and a little cayenne. Cover very close. Stew till perfectly tender then squeeze a lime or lemon over it in a dish. Rice may be served as with curry.

1873

"The great secret of cooking a steak consists in making a roaring fire, and then adding some coke to it. When this is red-hot you have a clear smokeless fire on which to cook your steak. You should cook it on the fire, and not in front of it, otherwise it is only a toasted bit of meat, instead of a broiled steak. How long you are to leave a steak on the fire is so entirely a question of judgment as well as a matter of taste, that it is impossible to give any rule about it. You should turn your steak as soon as it has been on the fire a few minutes, and keep turning it till it is done. This process prevents the formation of a hard rind of overdone meat. For a steak to be well cooked it ought to be equally done throughout its thickness, but not by any means overdone, and consequently dry. There are people, however, who abominate a juicy steak, and will have their meat in any form thoroughly done, or rather overdone, not to say actually spoilt."

Bubble and squeak

Cold salt meat is slightly fried in a pan and cold cabbage is warmed, after having been cut into pieces and a little salt and pepper put on it. The fried cabbage is then dished up and garnished with the beef. It is desirable that the boiled beef should be rather underdone before it is again warmed through in the pan.

Beef a la mode

Take any fleshy piece of beef, remove the bone, lard it all over with unsmoked bacon and dust it with finely minced parsley and chives, salt, ground pepper, and other spices. Take a saucepan, into which put a small quantity of ordinary white wine (good cider does well as a substitute), bacon cut small into dice, shallots minced fine, small onions whole, slices of carrots, peppercorns, and a little salt. Lay your beef upon these ingredients, cover the stew pan close, and put it over a slow fire. Make it simmer gently for five or six hours, and then serve your beef with all its accompaniments and seasonings.

1884

"The effect of keeping game is not only to make it tender, but likewise to bring out its flavour. Nothing is more tasteless than a pheasant cooked too soon, or has finer a flavour after hanging a proper length of time."

Juicy corned beef

To enjoy corned beef juicy after it is cold and not as dry as a chip, put it into boiling water. Remove from heat and do not take it out of the pot until it is cold.

Roast lamb quarter

Lard the lamb on the thin side with small pieces of bacon, and sprinkle the other part with bread crumbs. When almost done, take it from the fire and sprinkle it a second time with crumbs of bread, seasoned with salt and parsley. Put the joint down to brown, and when done serve with sharp sauce.

Fried veal and oyster patties

Mince a bit of cold veal and six oysters, mixed with a few crumbs of bread, salt, pepper, nutmeg, and the very smallest bit of lemon peel. Add the liquor of the oysters, warm all in a tosser but do not boil. Let it get cold. Have ready a good puff pastry, roll thin, and cut into round or square bits. Put some of the above between two of them, twist the edges to keep in the gravy. Fry them to a fine brown. May also be baked.

Trotters a la poulette

Take a little good stock into a stew pan. Thicken it with a mixture of the yolk of an egg, cream or milk, butter, and a very little flour. Add pepper or Cayenne, lemon juice, or Chili vinegar, salt, white onions boiled tender and well mashed. Heat the prepared trotters in this till cooked. Serve with just enough of the sauce, boiled up and thickened, to cover then. This dish is largely consumed in Paris.

Calf's brains a la maître d'hôtel

Take off all the fibres and skins which hang about the brains, and soak them several times in water. Boil them in salt and water, with a piece of butter and a tablespoonful of vinegar. Cut some thin slices of bread in the shape of scallop shells, and fry them in butter. Lay these in a dish and put the brains divided in two on them, and pour over Maître d'hôtel sauce, which is made in the following manner: Put a piece of butter into a saucepan with some hashed parsley, some tarragon leaves, one or two leaves of balm, with salt, lemon, or a glass of verjuice. Mix the whole with a wooden spoon until they are well incorporated.

Leftover roast beef pudding

Mince about a pound of cold leftover beef. Add to it one teaspoonful of salt, the same of flour, and half the quantity of pepper. Mix well. Fill pastry with the prepared meat, and add a gill of water. A little chopped onions and parsley may be added. Cover in the ordinary manner, shake well, and tie in a cloth. Boil for half an hour, or longer, if the pastry is thick.

Hashed mutton

Cut the remains of a cold leg or shoulder of mutton into thin slices, whether fat or lean, flour and pepper well, and leave in the dish. Boil the bones, well broken up, with a few onions minced well, add some salt, a little mushroom catsup, and the hashed meat. Warm over a slow fire, but do not let it boil. Then add port wine and currant jelly, or omit, as you please. If the former, it will impart a venison flavour; if the latter method is adopted it will be plain.

Roast tripe

Cut it into oblong pieces, and having made a forcemeat of bread crumbs, chopped parsley, pepper and salt, with the yolks of two eggs, lay it on the tripe. Put the pieces together, roll tightly, and tie. Roast it for an hour and a half, basting well with butter; serve it with melted butter or a little sharp sauce.

Dutch fricandel

Take two and a half pounds of veal and a quarter of pound of suet, chop both fine, as if making sausage-meat. Add three eggs beaten well, a nutmeg ground, and pepper and salt to taste. Soak a slice of bread in boiling milk, mix the whole well together with a little flour. Bake for two hours and a half in a moderate oven, or until its pale brown but it should not have a hard crust on top.

Sheep's tongues in paper

Scald, peel, and stew with vegetables, the tongues which you require to serve. If you have only one or two, you may boil them in your soup kettle. When they are done quite enough, split them in two and let them cool. Smear them with butter, into which fine chopped sweet herbs have been worked; season with pepper, salt, and allspice. Wrap each half tongue in oiled paper, broil them over a gentle fire, and serve very hot, without taking them out of the paper.

Chine of pork, roasted

Make a stuffing of parsley, thyme, sage, eggs, and crumbs of bread, seasoned with pepper and salt, shallot, and nutmeg. Let it be stuffed thick, and roasted gently. When about one-fourth roasted cut the skin into long strips. Serve with potatoes and apple sauce.

Concentrated beef

Concentrated beef is invaluable in barren regions. It may not be generally known that the substance of thirty or forty pounds weight of meat reduced to a single pound of gelatine, compressed into a sausage is very portable, and a few shavings of it will make a rich soup. It may be effected by it very simple process of boiling, then evaporating and skimming off the fat, and finally reducing it over a slow fire to a thick substance, which might be poured into any air tight vessel, being first seasoned. When cold it would become a firm mass. Any house wife might easily perform the operation, and it is believed to be within the culinary powers of a hut keeper, who might thus provide a pleasing, and generous change to the eternal beef and damper, damper and beef, and an enterprising cook, who would introduce such a condiment in the bush, would be deserving the golden opinions of all residents there.

Poultry

Giblet pie

After very nicely cleaning goose or duck giblets, stew them with a small quantity of water, onion, black pepper and a bunch of sweet herbs, till nearly done. Let them stand till cold and if not enough to fill the dish lay beef, veal, or two or three mutton steaks at the bottom. Put the liquor of the stew to bake with the above, and when the pie is baked pour in a teaspoonful of cream if it is to be had. Sliced potatoes added to it eat extremely well.

Cock-a-leekie

Boil from four to six pounds of good shin beef, well broken, till the liquor is very good. Strain it and put in a capon or large fowl, trussed as for boiling. When it boils, add half the quantity of leeks intended to be used, well cleaned, and cut in inch lengths, or longer. Skim this carefully. In half an hour add the remaining leeks, and a seasoning of pepper and salt. The soup must be very thick of leeks, and the first part of them must be boiled down into the soup until it becomes a lubricous compound. Sometimes the capon is served in the tureen with the soup. Some people thicken cock-a-leekie with oatmeal flour. Those who dislike so much of the leeks may substitute with greens or spinach.

Stewed fowl and rice

Stew the fowl on very low heat in some clean mutton broth. Skim well and season with onions, mace, pepper and salt. About half an hour before it is ready, put in half a cup of rice, well washed and soaked. Simmer until tender, then strain it from the broth and put the rice through a sieve. Before the fire, keep the fowl hot. Lay it in the middle of the dish, and put the rice round it without the broth. The broth will be very nice as such but the less liquor the fowl is done with the better. Use parsley and butter for sauce.

Roasted duck

Stuff the duck with a mixture of sage, onion, a dessertspoonful of bread crumbs, a bit of butter and salt and pepper. Roast in oven or in sealed stew pan over the fire. Serve with gravy.

Stewed chicken with wine

Take two or three chickens (if small) wash them clean from the blood, and joint them. Set them on the fire in as much water as will cover them. When they boil up, skim them and then take them out and strain the liquor. Take the liquor and put in some pepper whole and ground, a blade or two of mace, salt to taste, a little lemon peel, a small onion stuck with three or four cloves, a quarter of a pint of white wine warmed. Then add the chicken. Boil all these together till the chickens are done enough. Then add three tablespoonfuls of cream (a little flour mixed with it). Stir it well over the fire till it begins to thicken then take the yolk of two eggs, well beaten and flavoured with a little nutmeg and juice of lemon. Mix these by degrees with the liquor very carefully for fear of curdling. Then put in a half pound of good butter and shake it together till melted.

Chicken rissoles

Chop the white part of chicken that has been dressed, or any white meat. Add a little lemon juice, grated lemon peel, onion, white pepper, salt, nutmeg, and mace. Mix all with a little butter and a spoonful of cream. Wrap the mince up in a thin puff pastry in the form of balls or sausages. Rub them over with the yolk of an egg and cover them with bread crumbs grated very fine. Fry until a light brown, and serve them with crimped parsley. They may be done without pastry, but must be mixed up with an egg to bind the mince, and be wetted with another on the surface, as they require more crumb. Croquets may be made of the same ingredients as rissoles, but rolled into a thin paste of flour and water, then fried.

Duck hash

Cut cold duck into joints and warm through in gravy (without boiling). Add a glass of port wine, a teaspoonful of mustard and a little butter and flour.

1853

"Dinner time is fast approaching. One digger is heaping fresh coals around and on the top of the camp oven, in which a joint of meat is baking, resting on a piece of iron hoop to keep it from the bottom and preserve it from a burnt flavour. Another has completed a dozen rounds of damper, made in the gold washing dish, of flour and water and a little soda or yeast made from flour and sugar and water, which he will bake in the hot wood ashes."

Chicken or fowl salad

Trim neatly the remains of cold roast or boiled chicken. Wash, dry, and slice two lettuces, and place in the middle of the dish. Put the pieces of fowl on the top, and pour salad dressing over them. Garnish the edge of the salad with hard boiled eggs cut in rings, sliced cucumber, and boiled beetroot cut in slices. Instead of cutting the eggs in rings the yolks may be rubbed through a sieve, and the whites chopped very finely, and arranged on the salad in small bunches, yellow and white alternately.

Boiled duck

Choose a fat duck and salt it for two days. Then boil it slowly in a cloth. Serve with onion sauce but melt the butter with milk instead of water.

Chicken curry

A fowl is cut up into small pieces. Take four dried and two green onions, five chilies, half a turmeric, one teaspoon of coriander seed, one of white cumin, and one of sweet cumin. You must well pound the seeds, turmeric and cumin. Slice the onions fine then take the saucepan, and after buttering it, lightly brown the onions, then add the pounded ingredients with just sufficient water to reduce them to a paste, and throw in the fowl and well mix them up till the meat has a yellow tint. Lastly, add coconut milk and boil till the curry be thoroughly cooked. Coconut milk is made by scraping the meat of half of an old nut very fine, then soaking it in warm water, and after squeezing out the milk, throw the fibre away.

Seafood

Salmon with white sauce

Having cut the salmon in slices, melt some butter in a saucepan, and put in a little salt. Rub the slices of salmon with this butter and broil them over a slack fire. Make white sauce as follows: take some butter and put it into a saucepan with a pinch of flour and a couple of minced anchovies. Add some capers and a whole leek. Season with salt, pepper and nutmeg. Put in a little water, and a drop of vinegar. When the salmon is broiled on one side, turn it to the other. Then sauce should be constantly stirred and when it is due thickness, put it into the dish upon which you intend to serve the salmon. Take out the leek, lay in the slices of salmon. Serve warm.

Trumpeter whiting

This is, without exception the finest flavoured fish in the Southern Hemisphere, and is said to rival turbot in delicacy. Take five or six pounds and boil it in salted water. Serve with plain butter, for a pungent sauce overcomes the delicate taste. It is good fried, salted and smoked, but the simple boil is by far the most sensible mode of dressing this fish. When cleaning the fish, the flavour is much improved by adding a little salt and vinegar to the last water through which they are passed.

Potato and fish cakes

One pound of cooked fish, one pound of potatoes, the yolk of an egg, a little cayenne. Mash the potatoes well. Mix all thoroughly in the mortar. Form into small cakes, dip in egg and bread crumbs and fry.

Lobster or crab cutlets

Take out the meat of either a lobster or crab and mince it up. Add two ounces of butter, browned with one tablespoonful of flour, and seasoned with a little pepper, salt, and cayenne. Add about half a pint of strong stock. Stir the mixture over the fire until quite hot, and lay it in separate tablespoonsful on a large dish. When they are cold form them into the shape of cutlets, brush them over with the yoke of an egg (beaten). Dip them in bread crumbs and then fry them of a light brown colour in clarified beef dripping. Place round a dish, with a little fried parsley in the centre.

Eel pie

After skinning them, cut the eels in lengths of two or three inches. Season with pepper and salt, and place in the dish with some bits of butter and a little water. Cover with pastry and bake. Middle sized eels do best.

Oyster and sweetbread pie

As you open the oysters, separate them from the liquor. Remove the beards. Strain the liquor and in it parboil the oysters. Parboil sweetbreads, and cutting them in slices, lay them and the oysters in layers. Season very lightly with salt, pepper and mace. Then pour over half a teacup of liquor and the same of gravy. Bake in a slow oven. Before you serve, put a teacup of cream, a little more oyster liquor, and a cup of white gravy, all warmed but not boiled.

Oyster fritters

Make a stiff batter with one or two eggs and a little flour, according to the quantity required. Season to taste with pepper and salt. Prepare some oysters as if for sauce, dip each in the batter, and fry of a nice brown colour, either in very fresh lard or butter. Lay them on a clean sieve before the fire, until every particle of grease has drained from them. Serve them on a hot napkin.

Crayfish

Boil a pint of milk, two blades of mace, one onion sliced, cayenne, and salt, with lemon, a little butter and flour and a gill of cream. Serve over boiled crayfish.

Cod pie

Take a piece of the middle of a cod and salt it well over night. Next day wash it, season with pepper, salt, and a very little nutmeg. Place in a dish and put some butter on it and a little water. Cover it with crust pastry. Oysters may added. Bake.

1886

"It frequently happens that good yeast cannot be got, although a chemical leaven, in the shape of potent yeast, is now very common. When, however, the yeast has been touched with the weather, mix a little flour and sugar with it, and allow it to work before mixing it with the dough."

Baked pike with oyster

Bake the fish. Beard and mince oysters, prepare and mix three ounces of bread crumbs, one teaspoonful of minced savoury herbs, two anchovies (these may be dispensed with), two ounces of suet, salt, pepper, and pounded mace to taste. Add six tablespoonfuls of cream or milk, the yolk of two eggs, blending all well together. Moisten with cream and eggs, put all into a stew pan. Stir it over the fire till it thickens, then put onto the fish, which should have previously been cut open, and serve it up.

Persian kedgeree

One pound of cooked fish, chopped fine. A quarter pound of rice boiled as for curry. Two eggs hard boiled and finely chopped. Two ounces butter, a little cayenne, salt. Mix well together in a saucepan till thoroughly heated. Put lightly on a dish, or in a mould. Very good with poached eggs.

Minced crab

Remove the meat, mince small and place in a saucepan with a glassful of white wine. Add pepper and nutmeg, Cayenne pepper, and two spoonfuls of vinegar. Let it stew for a minutes. Melt a piece of butter the size of a hen's egg, with an anchovy and the yolks of two eggs. Beat it up and mix in with the crab. Add sufficient stale breadcrumbs to thicken. Garnish with thin toast cut with a pastry leaf cutter, and the claws, and parsley. Lobster be dressed in the same manner.

Collared salmon

Spilt enough of the fish to make a handsome roll. Wash, and wipe it well, rub the inside and outside well with powdered white pepper, mace, salt, and Jamaica pepper, carefully mixed. Roll it tight and bind it up. Put as much water and one-third of vinegar as will cover it, add salt, long pepper, allspice, and two bay leaves. Cover it close and simmer till done enough. Drain and boil the liquor quickly, and pour it over the fish when cold. Serve with fennel.

Game

Stewed pigeon

Take three pigeon, with their giblets. Cut the pigeons in quarters and put them in the stew pan with two slices of mace, a little pepper and salt, and just water enough to stew them without burning When they are tender thicken the liquor with the yolk of one egg, a tablespoonful of cream, a bit of butter, and a little shred of thyme and parsley, shake them all up together and garnish with lemon.

Emu

The best time to hunt for Emu is in the morning when they are cropping for grasses otherwise they are swift of foot. The rump, which can be roasted or boiled and resembles coarse beef in flavour. It is best served with a sauce.

Roast kangaroo

The hind quarters of a medium sized brush Kangaroo is to be larded with bacon and put down to roast. It must be well basted and stuffed with a good veal stuffing. Serve with gravy and currant jelly. It can be basted with good dripping or milk – the latter is best.

1879

Napoleon was so taken with this meat as fare, he wanted to stock his estate with Kangaroo. They were fetching as much £10 per pair in Paris.

Sticker up spitted kangaroo

Take Kangaroo, a piece of which is divided nicely into cutlets, two or three inches thick. Then take a straight clean stick, about four feet long, sharpened at both ends. On the narrow part of this, for the space of a foot or more, the cutlets are spitted at intervals and on the end placed a piece of rosy fat bacon. The strong end of the stick is now stuck fast into the ground, close by the fire, to leeward, care being taken that it does not burn. Then the bacon on the summit of the spit, speedily softening in the blaze, drops a rich and savoury lubricating shower upon the leaner kangaroo cutlets below.

Hashed venison or kangaroo

Cut the meat into slices. Put it in a stew pan with a small quantity of stock gravy, a gill of port wine, a tablespoon of ketchup, some lemon, with salt and cayenne in moderation. Let it simmer. Serve in a hot dish with currant jelly.

Kangaroo steamer

Take the tenderest part of the Kangaroo, being careful to remove all the sinews. Chop it very fine. Add about the same quantity of bacon. Season with finely powdered marjoram, pepper and a very little salt. Let it steam or stew for two hours. Serve with gravy that has been flavoured with mace, salt and pepper.

1851

"Emigrants from the country, especially those who have very young children, might add much to their comfort by carrying with them a few bottles of milk of their own preparing. The process is easy, and the effect certain. Put the milk into bottles, well corked. Put these into a pan with cold water, and gradually raise it to the boiling point. Take it from the fire and let the bottles cool in the water in which they were boiled. The milk will remain perfectly sweet for upwards of six months. In Italy they carry the process further in the production of a dry substance called Latteina. Instead of putting the milk in bottles, they evaporate it to dryness, under constant stirring. A dry mass is thus obtained, which, when dissolved in water, is said to possess all the properties of the best milk. A little practice of this method would not be thrown away by the intending emigrant"

Slippery bob

Take Kangaroo brains and mix with flour and water, and make into a batter. Well season with pepper and salt. Then pour a tablespoonful at a time into an iron pot containing emu fat and take them out when done. It requires a good appetite and excellent digestion.

Wild duck

Keep them sufficiently, and roast them rather under done, not forgetting to baste well. Serve with lemon, port wine sauce and cayenne pepper. When carving, be sure to slice the breast, and pour over the cuts a few spoonfuls of sauce as opposed to port wine or warmed claret.

Hare

Some fill the belly with forcemeat, but if the hare is tender don't do so. Put it down to roast, away from the fire at first, but afterwards draw nearer and keep eternally basting with milk or cream, and subsequently with butter. Mince the liver, and flour the hare well when nearly done, so as to raise to a froth on the joint. Served hot with red currant jelly.

Hare soup

Take the fillets of two hares and cut into small pieces. Fry them in butter. Chop the rest of the hare and all the bones and put them in a stew pan with a bunch of sweet herbs, a few cloves, mace, onions, celery, pepper, and salt to the taste. Let it boil gently for four hours, then strain it off, and have some good strong beef stock to add to the soup. Thicken it with boiling butter and flour, put two large tablespoonful of mushroom catsup and one of Indian soy. Put the pieces of fried hare into the soup and let it boil five minutes. Ground rice or the blood of the hare is the Scotch mode of thickening.

Rabbit pie

Cut a nice rabbit into joints, splitting the head in halves, and lay them in lukewarm water half-an-hour to disgorge, then dry them upon a cloth. Season well with pepper, salt, chopped eschalots, parsley, two bay leaves, and a spoonful of flour. Have ready also three-quarters of a pound of uncooked and streaked bacon, cut into square pieces the size of walnuts. Build up the pieces of rabbit and bacon together in a pie dish, commencing with the worst piece, and forming a dome. Pour in a little water, cover with pastry and bake.

Roman pie

Take one boiled rabbit, or an equal quantity of any lean white meat, cut into neat pieces. Butter a baking dish and sprinkle it thickly with vermicelli, then line it with a plain pastry. Pack into it the meat, some ham cut in small pieces, two ounces macaroni boiled quite tender and cut into little bits, one half ounce of vermicelli broken and also boiled, two ounces grated cheese, a very little finely chopped onion and parsley, pepper and salt, and not quite half a pint of cream. Cover it carefully with pastry and bake an hour. Turn it out to serve.

Fricasseed rabbit

Brown some bacon, slice in a stew pan with a good lump of butter. Take it out of the stew pan and put your rabbit in. Brown it nicely all over, as far as you can, and then put back to it the bits of bacon. Throw in a dessertspoonful of flour, moisten gradually with broth and white wine. Season with pepper and salt. Add small onions. Serve with fried and toasted bread, laid on as garnishing around the dish.

Soups & stews

Macaroni soup

Boil one pound of the best macaroni in a quart of good stock till tender. Then take out half and put it into another stew pan. To the remainder add some more stock and boil it till you can pulp the macaroni through a fine sieve. Then add altogether the two liquors, a pint or more of cream boiling hot, the macaroni that first taken out, and a half a pound of grated Parmesan cheese. Make it hot, but do not let it boil. Serve it with the crust of a French roll cut into pieces the size of a shilling. Stock can be veal or beef. Grated parmesan cheese may be served over top.

Giblet soup

Scald and clean three or four sets of goose or duck giblets. Set them to stew, with a pound or two of gravy beef, scrag of mutton, or the bone of a knuckle of veal. Add three onions, a large bunch of sweet herbs, a teaspoonful of white pepper and a large spoonful of salt. Put five pints of water, and simmer till the gizzards (which must be in each four pieces) are tender. Skim nicely, and add a quarter of a pint of cream, two teaspoons of mushroom powder, and an ounce of butter mixed with a dessertspoonful of flour. Let it boil a few minutes, and serve with the giblets. It may be seasoned, instead of cream, with two glasses of sherry or Madeira, a large spoonful of ketchup, and some cayenne. When in the tureen add salt.

1853

"There are many ways of furnishing a house and those about to marry could derive a few hints as to what they can do without from the diggings, where, in a quarter of an hour a man can pack up, take his house, bedding, furniture, domestic utensils and provisions on his back, and start off on a forty mile expedition."

Clam soup

When the season is near at hand and when the market supplied with clams, the following recipe for making clam soup cannot be surpassed. Boil for three hours a knuckle of veal, with a goodly portion of water, and one onion. Strain and add the liquor of fifty clams. Thicken with a tablespoonful of flour, well rubbed with butter, the size of a small egg. Have your clams cut in three pieces, with the hard rind removed. Beat the yolks of two eggs very light, and put into a tureen with chopped parsley and a half-pint of milk. Just before serving drop the clams into the boiling soup, letting them boil up once. Put into tureen, stirring well its contents while doing so.

Soup maigre

Melt half a pound of butter in a stew pan, shake it round. Throw in six onions sliced. Shake the pan well for two or three minutes then put to it five heads of celery, two cabbage lettuces cut into small pieces. Add some parsley. Stir well for ten minutes. Then put in two quarts of water, some crusts of bread, a teaspoon of ground pepper, three or four blades of mace and if you have any white beet leaves, cut them into small pieces and add a large handful. Boil gently for an hour. Just before serving beat in two egg yolks and a large spoonful of vinegar.

Mutton mock turtle

Stew one and a half pounds of scrag of mutton in three pints of water. Then set the broth on, with a calf's foot or cow heel, cover the stew pan tight and simmer till you can get the meat from the bones in proper bits. Set the broth and pieces of meat on again, add a quarter of a pint of Madeira wine or sherry, a large onion, half a teaspoonful of cayenne pepper, a bit of lemon peel, two anchovies, some sweet herbs, eighteen oysters (cut into pieces then chopped fine), a teaspoonful of salt, a little nutmeg, and the liquor of the oysters. Cover it tight and simmer for half an hour. Serve with forcemeat balls and small eggs in the tureen.

Small eggs for mock turtle

Beat three hard egg yolks and one raw egg yolk in a mortar to make into a paste. Roll it into small balls, and throw them into boiling water for two minutes to harden.

Forcemeat for mock turtle

A pound of fine fresh suet, one ounce of ready dressed veal or chicken chopped fine, crumbs of bread a little shallot or onion salt, white pepper, nutmeg, mace, penny royal, parsley, grated lemon, and finely shredded thyme. Beat as many fresh eggs (yolks and whites separately) as will make the above ingredients into a moist paste. Roll into small balls, and fry them in fresh lard, putting them in just as it boils up. When light brown take them out and drain them before the fire. If the suet be moist or stale, a great many more eggs will be necessary. Balls made this way are remarkably light, but being greasy, some people prefer them with less suet and eggs.

1862

"Cookery is a great art, but it gives us only new flavours, and people want a new meat. The poor have sauces which makes all food pleasant, but the middle class would welcome a change from the three sorts of meat which, with common poultry, form the staple of their flesh diet. While even the rich, who have the advantage of many sorts of game, and one or two kinds of scarce flesh, sigh for some food which shall be at once novel and procurable all the year round."

Veal mock turtle

Into a pan, put a knuckle of veal, two fine cow heels, two onions, a few cloves, some peppercorns, berries of allspice, mace, and sweet herbs. Cover them with water, then tie with a thick paper over the top. Bake it in the oven for three hours. When cold, take off the fat very nicely. Cut the meat and feet into pieces an inch and a half square, remove the bones and coarse parts. Then put the rest on to warm. Add a large spoonful of walnut and one mushroom ketchup, half a pint of sherry or Madeira wine, a little mushroom powder, and the jelly of the meat. When hot, if it wants any seasoning, add some. Serve with hard boiled eggs, forcemeat balls, a squeeze of lemon and a spoonful of soy.

Another Method - Bespeak a calf's head with the skin on, cut it in half, and clean it well. Then half boil it, take off all the meat in square bits, break the bones of the head, and boil them in some veal and beef broth to add to add to the richness. Fry some shallots in butter, and dredge them with flour enough to thicken the gravy. Stir this into the browning, and give it one or two boils. Skim it carefully, and then put in the head. Put in also a pint of Madeira wine, and simmer till the meat is quite tender. About ten minutes before you serve, put in some basil, tarragon, chives, parsley, cayenne pepper, and salt to taste. Add two spoonfuls of mushroom ketchup and one of soy. Squeeze the juice of a lemon into the tureen, and pour the soup upon it, forcemeat balls, and small eggs.

Pumpkin soup

Take part of a pumpkin, pare off the skin and remove the seeds. Cut it into small pieces. Place them in a stew pan on the fire, with some water. When the pumpkin is pulped, put in about half a quarter pound of butter and a little salt. Boil a quart of milk, and mix it in with the pumpkin pulp. Put some bread, cut in thin slices, in the tureen and pour the hot soup over it.

Cock a leekie soup

Boil four pounds of lean beef until the liquor is good. Take out the meat and put into the soup a fowl cut into pieces, with half the quantity of leeks intended to be used. Let it simmer and half an hour before serving, add the remainder of the leeks and season with salt and pepper.

1872

"Every kind of vegetable intended to be served whole should, when put to boil, be placed at once in boiling water and this applies especially to potatoes and vegetables from which the outer cover has been removed. Now it often happens that potatoes, etc, are, to save time, placed in cold water and left to boil gradually. It is just this which allows the nutritious matter to escape and renders the meal unsatisfying. When, on the contrary, the water boils from the moment the vegetable is immersed in it, the albumen is partially coagulated near the surface, and serves to retain the virtue of the vegetable. The reverse is, of course, the rule for making soup, or any dish from which the water will not be drained. By placing the vegetables in cold water the albumen is slowly dissolved, and actually mixes with the water - a process most necessary for the production of nutritious soup."

Hare soup

Take a hare and cut it in pieces, put into an earthen dish, with two onions cut small, three blades of mace, a pinch of salt, two anchovies, or three quarters of a red herring, three quarts of water, and wine to flavour, perhaps a pint of red wine. Bake in a quick oven for three hours, then strain the liquor into a stew pan. Have ready boiled four ounces of fine pearl barley, add this. Scald the liver, and rub it through a sieve with a wooden spoon. Put this into the soup, set over the fire and keep stirring till near boiling, but it must not boil. Then remove. Put some toasted bread into the tureen, pour on the soup and serve hot.

Irish stew

Take about two pounds of coarse beef, the cheaper part, if perfectly fresh, answers well and the cost of it very moderate. Remove some of the fat if overmuch. Cut the meat into small pieces, and put them into an earthenware baking pot with two or three onions and a carrot, both to be sliced. Add two teaspoonful's of salt and one of pepper. Pour over a pint and a half of water. Put on the lid on the pot and let the whole stew in the oven for one hour. Then cover the stew with pared potatoes, and return the pot to the oven. Cover the top of it as before, and let the stew cook for another hour and a half, when the potatoes will be a pulp. Turn on to a hot dish and serve at once.

Pea soup

To make pea soup you must first soak the peas overnight in a pint of water. Then put them on to simmer in two quarts of water with some mutton bones, two heads of celery, a sprig of savoury and a little sweet marjoram, pepper and salt. Let it simmer for an hour. Add and onion cut small. When nearly done, take out the mutton bones and add a pound of bacon, cut into little pieces. Serve with toasted bread and powdered mint. Pea soup is invariably made first rate on board ship.

Vegetable soup

Peel and slice six large onions, six potatoes, six carrots and four turnips. Fry them in a half-pound of butter, and pour on them four quarts of boiling water. Toast a crust of bread as brown and as hard as possible, but do not burn it. Put some celery, sweet herbs, white pepper, and salt, to the above and then stew it all gently for four hours. Then strain it through a coarse cloth. Have ready sliced carrot, celery, and a little turnip, and add to your liking. Stew them tender in the soup. If approved, you may add an anchovy and a spoonful of ketchup.

Ox tail soup

Take two large or three small tails, divide them completely at the joints, rub them with salt, and soak well in warm water. Remove after they have soaked for an hour and a half, and place in a stew pan with a faggot of parsley, four or five onions, a dozen peppercorns, a blade of mace, a turnip, and two carrots sliced, and three quarts of water. Stew gently for two and a half hours, or until the meat is tender, then remove, cut into small pieces. Place the meat in a fresh stew pan. Thicken the soup with a little browned flour, rubbed up with a ladleful of the top fat, and then strain it into the stew pan containing the tails. Boil up, skim well, add mushroom catsup and pepper to taste. Serve hot.

Palestine soup

Put two ounces of butter into a stew pan, add fifteen Jerusalem artichokes washed and peeled, four onions, two sticks of celery, half a pound of lean ham and a little salt. Slice all these ingredients, and stew them until soft in the butter, then add a quart of good white stock, with a small bit of mace. Boil gently for half an hour. Pulp it through a sieve and let it stand till next day. When ready to serve, put in half a pint of thick cream.

Soup kitchen soup

To seventy gallons of cold water put forty pounds of rice, ten pounds of sago and ten pounds of barley. Boil for one hour and mash well. Add fourteen pounds of Indian meal, fourteen pounds of oatmeal and five pounds of salt mixed with a little water. Add fourteen pounds of flour mixed with cold water. Boil for a half hour. Add eight pounds of treacle and a half pound of pimento mixed in warm water.

Vegetables & accompaniments

Potato wall

This is an accompaniment or edging to a fricassee of fish. Mash in a mortar as many potatoes as you want, with a good piece of butter. Then with the bowls of two silver spoons raise a wall of it two inches and a half high within the rim of the dish to be used. Let the upper part be a little thinner than the lower. Smooth it and after brushing it all over with egg, put it into the oven to become hot and a little coloured.

Pickled nasturtiums

Gather them young. Lay them in salt and water for one night. Drain, then cover them with hot vinegar, boiled with a little black and Jamaica pepper. A couple of capsicums put into the jar are a great improvement.

New potatoes

Well wash them, rub off the skins with a course cloth. Put them into boiling water, salted in proportion of one tablespoon of salt to half a gallon of water. Let them boil until tender – try them with a fork. When done, pour out the water and let them stand by the side of the fire with the lid of the sauce pan partially uncovered. When the potatoes are dry put them in a hot vegetable dish, with a piece of butter the size of a walnut.

Vegetable quarter

Wash a dish with egg white and make four divisions in it with fried bread. Put in each division the following vegetables. Stewed spinach in one, in the next mashed potatoes, in the third mashed turnips, and in the fourth blanched onions and sliced carrots, or pieces of cauliflower, or heads of broccoli.

Stewed cucumbers

Slice thickly or halve and divide them into two. Strew some salt and pepper and sliced onions. Add a little broth, or a bit of butter. Simmer very slowly. Before serving, if no butter was in before, put some and a little flour – or if there was butter then put in only a little flour unless it needs richness.

Potato pastey

Boil peeled and washed potatoes. Grate them as finely as possible and mix with salt, pepper and a good piece of butter. Make a pastry, roll it out thinly like a puff and put in the potatoes. Fold over one half and pinch the edges. Bake in a moderate oven

Peas pudding

Take a pint of split peas in a cloth, leaving them room to swell but not more. Put them into a stew pan of cold water and let them boil nearly half an hour until tender but not watery (which they would not be if allowed only sufficient room to swell and no more). Then turn them out of the cloth and rub them through a sieve into a basin. Add a quarter of a pound of butter, season with a little white pepper and salt and mix in three yolks and one whole egg. Lightly flour a pudding cloth and lay it in a small round-bottomed basin. Pour in the mixture, tie up the cloth and put the pudding to boil for an hour in a saucepan of boiling water. When done, turn it from the cloth upon a dish and serve with beef or pork.

Panada

Put the crumb of a grated penny loaf and a blade of mace into a quart of cold water. Set both on the fire. When it is boiled smooth, take it off the fire and put in a bit of lemon peel, the juice of a lemon, a glass of sack, and sugar to taste.

Norfolk dumplings

With a pint of milk, two well beaten eggs, and a little salt, mix as much flour as will make a thick batter. Drop a tablespoonful at a time into a stew pan of boiling water. A few minutes will do them. Take them up in a sieve to drain. Serve quickly with cold butter. The water must not cease boiling whilst they are doing.

Fricassee of parsnips

Boil parsnips in milk until they are soft then cut them lengthways into bits two or three inches long. Simmer in a white sauce, made of two spoonfuls of broth, a bit of mace, half a cup of cream, a bit of butter, some flour, pepper and salt.

1855

"A frugal little housewife can always, at a loss of about half an hour a day, supply bread for her family.

A bag of flour, weighing 200 pound, will cost at the present market rate, say 55s. This should turn out at least forty-seven loaves of four pounds each, though fifty should be the proper complement."

Preserved cucumbers

Pair and slice, as for eating, eight large cucumbers. Season well with pepper and salt, put them into a jar, with two or three small onions and as many shallots. Pour in a quart of vinegar. Cover close, and let it stand four days, then strain the vinegar through a sieve. Put it into four-ounce phials, and some whole pepper in each. Seal down the corks. The slices of cucumbers will keep in a jar closely covered without vinegar, and give a very agreeable flavour to hashes. Use in a winter salad or as a sauce for cold meat.

Cole cannon

Boil three large potatoes with their skins on. Peel them, bruise them to meal (mash), and mix them with three boiled and well drained cabbages. Add about half an ounce of butter, two spoonfuls of cream, pepper and salt. Heat and stir it over the fire and send it to table in the shape of a cake or in a mould.

Stewed celery

Wash six heads and strip off their outer leaves. Either halve or leave them whole, according to their size. Cut into lengths of four inches. Put them into a stew pan with a cup of broth or weak white gravy. Stew till tender then add two spoonfuls of cream and a little flour and butter seasoned with pepper, salt, and nutmeg. Simmer all together.

Cracknels

To a pint of flour take a half-pound of butter, a little grated nutmeg, the yolk of two eggs whisked with two spoons of rosewater; put the nutmeg and eggs into the flour, and wet it into a stiff paste with cold water then roll in the butter, and make them into shape; put them into a saucepan of boiling water, and when they rise take them out with a skimmer and put them into cold water; when they are hardened lay them out to dry, and bake them in tin plates.

Crisp parsley

When picked and washed very clean, put into a Dutch oven, or on a sheet of paper, and, keeping it at a moderate distance from the fire, turn it crisp.

Tomato salad

Peel half a dozen ripe tomatoes and slice them into a glass bowl. Make a mix of two pickled onions minced up, or a dessert spoonful of the vinegar from pickled onions, a dessert spoonful of Chili vinegar, and three tablespoonsful of salad oil. Add a dessert spoonful of powdered sugar. Mix well and pour over the tomatoes. Let them lie for ten minutes.

1853

"The more frugal owner of the adjoining tent is pouring the fat from his pan into a deep tin plate, adding a little pepper and salt, and thereby supplying himself with a butter quite equal to any the colony produces."

Cheese pudding

Grate three ounces of Parmesan cheese and five of bread, and having warmed one ounce of butter in a quarter of a pint of new milk, mix it with the above. Add two well-beaten eggs and a little salt. Bake it for half an hour.

Cayenne cheese biscuits

Take two ounces of flour, two ounces of grated cheese the same of butter, and a little Cayenne pepper. Mix them well together, roll into very thin biscuits, bake in a moderately heated oven, and serve hot.

Potato chips

Wash and peel some potatoes, then pare them, ribbon like into long lengths. Put them into cold water to remove the strong potato flavour. Drain them, and throw them into a pan with a little butter, and fry them a light brown. Take them out of the pan, and place them close to the fire on a sieve, lined with clean writing paper to dry before they are served up. A little salt may be sprinkled over them.

Macaroni

Put as much of the pipe to soak in cold water as you think proper, then boil it in milk and water till quite tender, with a small onion. When done, strain off the milk, and add a piece of butter the size of a walnut, a little cream, and some nutmeg. Mix well together, and put it into a dish, then cover with grated cheese, Parmesan or Cheshire. Put it in the oven or before the fire to be lightly browned, and serve hot with mustard.

Stewed tomatoes

Pour boiling water over the tomatoes, and remove the skins. Put them in the saucepan without any water, adding fresh butter, pepper, and salt, to your taste. Put in some bread-crumbs or pounded biscuit, and mash them as they stew. They will be done in a few minutes.

Baked tomatoes

Take large fine fruit, cut it up, and take out the seeds. Put the tomatoes in a deep dish, in alternate layers with pounded biscuit or bread-crumbs, with a little fresh butter, in small pieces, seasoned with salt and pepper. Finish with a layer of bread-crumbs, which should be plentifully used throughout. Bake slowly for two hours.

Preserved tomatoes

Prepare the fruit as for cooking, without seasoning. Boil for one hour then put them in small stone jars. Cork and boil the jars for two hours. Remove them from the fire; cork, and seal air-tight. When opened, season, and cook for half an hour.

1855

"In these cool days of our Australian winter, which seem to remind us of the early days of September in the old country, in favourable seasons, our thoughts sometimes wander back to the delicacies so common there, the frequent presents of a brace of partridges, and an occasional pheasant. We think that others too, not long enough away from the father land to forget its fashions, have had somewhat similar thoughts, and hence we find among our imports, marked "M & W, in diamond, 46 cases preserved game." Internally we apostrophised these merchants of Little Malop Street as happy men, and wondered whether they had, as in their place we would have done, reserved a sample case to give a keener relish to the day of rest; for be it wet or dry, the Sunday always to its seems bright."

Preserved green peas

Shell and put them into a kettle of water when it is boiling. Give them two or three turns only, and pour them into a colander. When the water drains off turn them on a dresser covered with cloth to dry perfectly. Then bottle them in wide-mouthed bottles, leaving only room to pour clarified mutton suet upon them an inch thick, and for the cork. Rest it down and keep in a cellar, or in the earth. When they are to be used, boil them till tender, with a bit of butter, a spoonful of sugar, and a bit of mint.

1880

The average wage for an Australian cook was about £40 per year. This was often more than double his or her counterparts in England.

Onions stuffed

Peel as many large onions as you require, cut a piece off at the top and bottom to give them a flat appearance, and which causes a bitter flavour if left. Blanch them in four quarts of boiling water for twenty minutes, then lay them on a cloth to dry. Take the middle out of each onion and fill them with veal forcemeat (with a little chopped eschalot, parsley, and mushroom mixed in it), and put them in a stew pan well-buttered. Cover them with white broth, let them simmer over a slow fire until covered with a glaze, and when tender turn them over. Serve when required.

Tomato pie

Take ripe nice tomatoes, remove the skins by pouring on boiling water. Line your plates with pastry, lay in the tomatoes in slices, sprinkle them with sugar, and add the juice and grated rind of a lemon. Cover, and bake about three-quarters of an hour for a deep pie.

Pickled tomatoes

Take the green fruit, the small round ones are to be preferred. Prick every one with a fork. Put into a brine with peppers, and then prepare and green, in the same way as cucumbers.

Balloon Potatoes

Take some large potatoes, peel them and cut them in slices, rather less than a quarter of an inch thick. Dry them thoroughly with a cloth, and put them in a frying basket. Have ready two pans filled with boiling lard. Plunge the basket in one and keeping shaking it. In two or three minutes lift up the basket and plunge it into the other pan, when the slices of potatoes will swell out; drain them of all fat and serve. The secret of success consists in removing the basket from the first pan of fat at the right moment. The potatoes should not be allowed to colour in it.

Boiled parsnips

When they are soft, take them up, scrape the dust off carefully, then scrape them all fine, lay in a saucepan with milk, and let them simmer till thick. Then add a piece of butter, and salt, and serve.

Baked German cauliflower

Boil the cauliflowers whole, in the usual way until nearly done enough. Drain well and arrange them as close together as possible on a dish that will stand the fire. Pour over them a thick sauce made of good broth, butter, flour, and nutmeg, with egg yolks stirred smoothly through. Dust over some grated Parmesan cheese, and bake half an hour in a not too fierce oven. On serving, the rim of the dish (well wiped) may be garnished with slices of fried sausages or smoked tongue.

1872

"The sheep is in its best condition as food when about five years old – an age which it is almost never allowed to attain, unless when intended for the private use of the owner and not for market. It is then sapid, full flavoured and firm, without being tough, and the fat has become hard. At three years old, as commonly procured from the butcher, it is well tasted, but is by no means comparable to that of five years. If younger than three years, it is deficient in flavour, and its flesh is pale. Meat which is half mutton and half lamb is very unpalatable food. Always choose mutton of a dark colour and marble like appearance."

Surprise eggs for parties

Separate in different vessels the yolks and whites of a sufficient number of eggs, stir any quantity of yolk together, from half a pint to a pint, or more. Put this into a bladder, tie up in a round form, and boil it hard. Then put this boiled yolk into another and larger bladder, into which pour the whites, keeping the hard yolk as much in the middle as possible. Tie the bladder in an oval form, and boil until the whole is quite hard. An immense egg may thus be formed, which, at a large dinner party, will surprise everyone, and may be used in a large dish of salad.

Egg toast

Have ready some hot buttered toast cut into quarters of rounds, according to the quantity required. Put a saucepan on the fire with some butter in it. As soon as melted, for a small dish break half-a-dozen eggs into the saucepan, with a little salt, and stir them well with a fork all the while they are on the fire, from five to ten minutes, according to its briskness. Lay a good tablespoonful of the eggs on each piece of toast, and serve.

Pork jelly

Take a leg of well-fed pork, beat it and break the bone. Set it over a gentle fire in 3 gallons of water, and simmer down to one gallon. Let an ounce of mace and an ounce of nutmeg stew along with it. Strain through a fine sieve, and when cold take off the fat. This is very good as a restorative for the weak.

Puff pastry

As a general rule, puff pastry requires one pound of butter to every pound of flour, half a salt spoon of salt and a little lemon juice, with about a quarter of a pint of the coolest water. The richer the pastry is made, the more lamiae of butter it contains, the more unwholesome, thus it can be made with half the quantity of butter. Put the flour onto the board and make a hole in the centre. In the hole put the yolk of one egg, lemon juice and salt. Mix the whole with cold water into a flexible paste.

Handle it as little as possible. Squeeze all the buttermilk from the butter, wring it through with a cloth. Roll out the paste. Place the butter on this and fold the edges of the paste over so as to hide it. Roll it out again to the thickness of a quarter of an inch; fold over one third top and bottom, thus forming a square. Roll out again and do the same twice over. Flour a baking sheet, put the paste on this and let it remain in a cool place for an hour. Then roll three times more, turning and folding it as before. After the paste has been rolled seven times it is ready for use. (In summer the water must be iced or cooled).

1853

"In making soup, the object desired is to get as much goodness out of the meat as possible. If, therefore, meat be put into boiling water the albumen in it immediately sets, coagulates, and forms an impermeable coating over the surface of the flesh, as the white of an egg does round the yoke, thus preventing the nutritive juices from being extracted by the water."

Sauces

Sauce piquante

Having fried your shallots, or onions, and a small clove of garlic and some sweet herbs, add equal parts of vinegar and water, or of vinegar and broth. Strain before serving.

Any condiments and flavours such as mushroom catsup, Worcester sauce, a tomato sauce, truffles, nutmeg, could be advantageously added to this sauce by a capable cook. Chopped gherkins are at times added to this sauce, and they much improve it.

Sage cream

Boil a quart of cream and add to it a quarter of a pint of the juice of the red sage, half a pint of sherry wine and half a pound of sugar.

Sharp sauce for venison, hare or kangaroo

A quarter pint of the best white wine vinegar and a quarter pound of white sugar. Let it simmer and serve.

Sauce Robert

This sauce is almost identical to Sauce Piquant, save in the addition of a small quantity of mustard, and if it be French, it be the better.

Sauce a la tartare

This sauce is almost identical to Sauce Robert and is produced using a larger quantity of mustard or gherkins. It is server cold.

Sauce poivrade

This sauce may be described as a plain sauce piquante without gherkins but in which pepper predominates.

Beef brose

After any large piece of beef has been taken out of the pot it was boiled in, skim off the fat with part of the liquor, and boil it in a saucepan. Have ready in a bowl oatmeal that has been toasted brown before the fire. Pour in the boiling liquor, and stir it a little. If too thick, add a little more liquor, and send it to table quite hot.

Fish sauce a la craster

Thicken a quarter pound of butter with flour and brown it. Then put to it one pound of best anchovies (cut small), six blades of mace, ten cloves, forty berries of black pepper, a few small onions, a bunch of sweet herbs, and a little parsley and sliced horseradish. On these pour half a pint of the best sherry, and a pint and a half of strong gravy. Simmer all gently for twenty minutes, then strain it through a sieve and bottle it for use. The way of using it is to boil some of it in the butter while melting.

Sauce for wild fowl

Simmer a teacupful of port wine, the same quantity of good meat gravy, a little shallot, a little pepper, salt, a grate of nutmeg and a bit of mace, for ten minutes. Put in a bit of butter and flour. Give it all one boil, and pour it over the birds. In general they are not stuffed, but may be done so if liked.

Bread sauce

Boil a large onion cut into four, with some black pepper and milk, till the onion is quite a pulp. Pour the milk strained, over grated white stale bread and cover it. In an hour put it into a saucepan, with a good piece of butter mixed with a little flour. Boil the whole up together and serve.

Sauce for rabbits

Boil the livers and shred them very small as well two eggs not boiled too hard. Add a large spoonful of grated bread. Have ready some strong beef stock and fresh herbs, and to a little of that add two tablespoons of white sugar and one of vinegar, a little salt and some butter; stir in all. Take care the butter does not oil, and shred the eggs very well.

1857

"It seems rather surprising that at a time so fertile in benevolent enterprises as ours, and when women showing an efficiency and zeal in many provinces of social service which will certainly mark the age this particular reform has not yet had its female apostle. One woman has virtually regenerated hospital nursing, another has instituted prison reform, another has organised Australian emigration, another has effectually restrained intemperance in a multitude of wild Californians, and another has regenerated the condition of lunatics in more countries than one. Why has no one re generated the cookery of the working classes, from the highest to the lowest?"

Wine sauce

Separate the yolk and whites of five eggs, beat them, and put them into a lined saucepan, add half a pint sherry, a quarter of a pint of water and two ounces of pounded sugar; place the saucepan over a sharp fire, and keep stirring until it begins to thicken; then take it off and serve. If it is allowed to boil it will be spoiled - it will immediately curdle. The above is sufficient for a large pudding. Allow about half the ingredients for a moderate-sized one.

Egg sauce

For sauce for half a dozen persons boil three eggs hard. When the eggs are quite cold chop them fine, and throw them into melted butter, which is thick of the butter and thin of the flour. A good dash of cream does no harm. Boil up and serve. If the fish with which the egg sauce is to be eaten has not been salted, it will be well to put a little salt in the sauce.

Dutch sauce

Put six spoonfuls of water and four vinegar into a saucepan. Warm and thicken with the yolks of two eggs. Make it quite hot, but do not boil it. Stir it continuously. Squeeze in the juice of half a lemon.

Hams or tongues glazing

Boil a shin of beef for twelve hours in eight or ten quarts of water. Draw the gravy from a knuckle of veal in the same manner. Put the same herbs and spices as if for soup, and add the whole to the shin of beef. It must be boiled till reduced to a quart. It will keep good for a year, and, when wanted for use, warm a little and spread over the ham, tongue, etc., with a feather.

Lobster sauce

Two eggs soft boiled for two minutes. With the soft part of the lobster add one half cup of drawn butter, one-half cup of vinegar, one teaspoonful of mustard, one half teaspoonful of black pepper. Scald together and stir constantly. When cold pour over the lobster.

Tomato ketchup

Scald and peel the fruit, as usual. Cover with salt and let it stand twenty-four hours. Then strain, and to every quart of the liquor and one half ounce of cloves, one ounce of ginger, one of pepper, one of black mustard seed, and two grated nutmegs. Boil half-an-hour, and add a pint of wine.

Gravy without any meat

Mix half a pint of beer, the same quantity of water, with pepper, salt, lemon peel, a couple of cloves and two spoonfuls of walnut or mushroom ketchup together. Flour and skin an onion or two and fry it in butter till brown. Then put the mixture into a stew pan, and simmer it for a quarter of an hour.

Oyster sauce

Open the oysters carefully, so as to preserve their liquor. Beard and remove the tough parts, then stew those parts in the liquor, adding sufficient water or veal broth to make the proper quantity of sauce. Allow for evaporation of about one-half. When done, strain it off and put it in a saucepan with the oysters, a teaspoonful of anchovy sauce, and a good-sized piece of butter rolled in flour. Keep turning it round to prevent the butter from curdling.

Sauce for boiled fish

Make ready while the fish is cooking, a tablespoonful of butter beaten to a cream, with a tablespoonful of browned flour, a pinch of salt and a pinch of pepper. Add the strained juice of one lemon and a teaspoonful of Worcestershire sauce or of any good vinegar from the pickle jar. Add a dash of red pepper, if you use the latter.

Beef stock

Take five pounds of lean beef, cut into small pieces. Put into pot or a digester, with sufficient water cover it. As it simmers, be careful to skim well. Add a faggot of herbs, and season with salt and ground pepper. When meat is tender, it may be moved from the pot, the stock skimmed well, the liquor strained through a fine sieve, and put aside in a covered pan for later use.

White sauce

Work the flour into the butter with a knife or spoon. Add a sufficient quantity of milk. Pour it into a saucepan, and let it just boil up. If it is wanted particularly rich, cream is used instead of milk.

Cakes, biscuits & breads

Shortbread

Rub one pound of butter and twelve ounces of finely powdered lump sugar into two pounds of flour, with the hands. Make it into stiff paste with four eggs. Roll out to double the thickness of a penny piece, cut it into round or square cakes, pinch the edges, stick slices of candied peel and some carraway comfits on the top, and bake them on iron plates in a warm oven.

Bread and butter pudding

Put thin slices of bread and butter without crust, spread apricot or orange marmalade on each slice. Lay them in a buttered mould or basin, and pour over a well-seasoned custard. Let it stand half an hour, then steam it for an hour. Serve with wine sauce.

Rook cakes

Put well together a pound and a half of flour, and half a pound of butter. Then add half a pound of fine sugar, half a pound of currants, four eggs, six tablespoonfuls of good cream, a wine glass of brandy, and a little water. When completely mixed, drop on to paper lumps about the size of a walnut, and bake in a slow oven.

Liquid Balm or Yeast

The following will be found an excellent recipe, by which bakers and others may manufacture their own yeast, in an expeditious and economical manner. Take one pound of concentrated extract of malt and hops, and mix it well into one gallon of boiling-hot water. Allow it to cool to 70° or 80°, and then add half-a-pint of common brewer's yeast. Now lay it aside to ferment. In twelve or fourteen hours it will be ready for immediate use, after rousing it well up, or it may he bottled, tying a piece of cloth over the neck, instead of using a cork. In a cool place, it will keep perfectly good a week or more. The liquid yeast thus prepared makes excellent bread, it does not cost half what is usually bought by the baker, and gives the bread a degree of tenacity not obtained from other yeast. One gallon, made as recommended, will raise two sacks of flour of twelve score each, equal to about one and a-half sacks of flour as would require 6 lbs. of the ordinary yeast.

Bread

Use twenty pounds of flour to make five loaves. The kneading trough should be kept solely for the purpose of making bread, and used for nothing else. The flour should be placed in this, and well hand rubbed to separate and break the lumps. The flour should then be heaped up in the centre from the sides of the trough.

In the middle of this a hole should be made, into which must be poured the yeast. For this quantity of flour half a pint will be enough, which must be mixed with about a pint of lukewarm water. When this has been poured into the hole, it should be stirred up with a spoon to mix a little of the flour with it, till it forms a thinnish batter. Over the surface of this, strew a little dry flour, and cover the whole with a cloth, placing the trough at such a distance from the fire as the climate and weather require, to keep it moderately heated.

When the crust on the top of the batter cracks, it is ready to begin to knead. This is to be done gradually, commencing with the part immediately round the yeast, adding more water, which should be lukewarm, till the whole is amalgamated. This is the nicest and most laborious part of the business, every particle of flour must be handled and mixed, or little dry lumps will appear in the baked loaves, and besides which, the yeast, to give regular and equal fermentation to the whole mass must be duly mixed throughout.

The salt can now be added - a handful will be sufficient - or when the water is being poured in. After the whole has been well kneaded, and worked with the fist, the whole should be rolled up into a lump, and dusted over with a little flour, covered over with a cloth to keep warm and to ferment.

After it has remained about twenty minutes or half-an-hour, it must be cut up into lumps, as near of a loaf size as possible, kneaded again separately, and placed in the oven. In about two hours the whole will be baked.

The great secret is to have your oven of the proper heat, and experience alone can guide a person in this matter, as much depends on the size and shape of the oven.

Twists, and fancy shaped loaves, of course can be made in an indefinite variety, but the principle is the same in their manufacture, excepting perhaps by the addition of a little carbonate of soda and milk, to make them light and spongy.

Earthen covered pots are the best to keep bread in, and that kneading-troughs should be made of the best seasoned Baltic pine, in preference to any other wood or material, unless it be English Elm or walnut.

1857

"Over a stretch of country large as Great Britain, the working man has an invariable diet which no stomach can long endure. Beefsteak three times a day, smoked and burnt outside and raw within, fried potatoes hard and greasy, and sometimes eggs ditto. Elsewhere it is salt pork fried - the most unwholesome diet, and nearly the most wasteful a man can sit down to. If husbands go on dining in this way for years together, it is only because there is no boarding house near where better fare is to be had. The table d'hôte is apt to sink to the level of the private house and then comes the catastrophe - universal indigestion, and unwholesome thirst, leading to drink and the barbarism which ensues."

Common teacake

Take ten eggs, half a pound of fresh butter, three quarters of a pound of wheaten flour, a quarter of a pound of rising flour, one and a half ounces of carraway seeds, one pound sifted loaf sugar, a small portion of volatile salts. Mode of mixing the above ingredients - the whites to be beaten separately from the yolks of the eggs, the latter also beat until the colour becomes pale then both mixed together, and beat up. The butter must be beaten until it comes to the consistency of thick cream, when it is added to the eggs, and again beaten up together. Meantime, the other ingredients should be made as dry as possible, either in the open air and sun or in a cool oven. When dry, these must be gradually mixed with the eggs and butter, keeping the mixture in a constant state of agitation, so that all may be intimately incorporated. As much volatile salts as will lie on the handle of a tea spoon is added, and also well mixed. It makes the cake light.

Amber Pudding

Beat well the yolks of four eggs, add a half a pound of butter melted, half a pound of melted sugar, and a little essence of lemon or ratafia to flavour it. Put pastry round the dish, and bake for half an hour.

Sweet potato fritters

Slice potatoes thin, dip them in fine batter and fry. Serve with white sugar sifted over them. Lemon peel and a spoonful of orange-flower water should be added to the batter.

Corn bread

Two cups of Indian corn meal, one cup flour, two eggs, a large spoonful of melted butter, two small teaspoons of cream of tartar, one of soda, and one of sugar. Mix well and bake.

Breakfast rolls

Boil one cup of curd milk with a cup of butter melted in. Make a hole in two quarts of flour and pour the milk. Add a quarter of a cup of sugar and half a cup of good yeast. Let it stand without mixing two or three hours. Salt to the taste then knead it. Set it to rise a few hours then mould it, and rise again in the pans before baking. The rolls require about fifteen minutes in a quick oven.

Gingerbread

A pound and a half of flour, one pound of treacle, three-quarters of a pound moist sugar, an ounce ground ginger, two ounces of caraway seeds, four ounces of citron and lemon peel candied, the yolks of four eggs. Cut the citron and lemon peel small, mix all the ingredients and bake it in large cakes on a tin plate.

Damper

Enough flour and water to make a pliable dough, and a little salt. Mix well, round into pieces and bake in fire ashes or set into a pan.

Preserved bread

Circumstances sometimes occur when it is desirable to keep bread for a long time. It may be done in the following manner. Cut the bread into thick slices and bake it in an oven so as to render it perfectly dry. In this condition it will keep good for any length of time required and without turning mouldy like ordinary bread. The bread thus prepared must, however, be carefully preserved from pressure otherwise, owing to its brittleness, it will soon fall to pieces. When required for use, it will only be necessary to dip the bread for an instant into warm water and then hold it before the fire to dry. Then butter it when it will taste like toast. This is a useful way of preserving bread for voyages, and also any bread that may be too stale to be eaten in the usual way.

Mince pies

Stone and cut two pounds of raisins, once or twice across, but do not chop them. Wash, dry, and pick three pounds of currants free from stalk and grit. Mince one and a half pounds of lean beef, and three pounds of suet, taking care that the latter is chopped very fine. Slice two ounces of citron and two ounces of candied lemon. Strain the juice of two lemons and mince the peel of one. Pare and core apples to fill two quarts when minced. When all the ingredients are prepared, mix them well together, adding half-a-pint of brandy when the other things are well blended. Press the whole into a jar, carefully exclude the air, and the mincemeat will be ready for use. When required, make some good puff pastry, roll it out to the thickness of a quarter of an inch, and line some good sized patty-pans with it. Fill them with mincemeat, cover with the pastry, and cat it off all round close to the edge of the tin. Put the pies into a brisk oven, to draw the pastry up, and bake for twenty-five minutes, or longer should the pies be very large. Brush them over with the white of an egg beaten with the blade of a knife to a stiff froth, sprinkle over pounded sugar, and put them into the oven for a minute or two to dry the egg. Serve hot.

Apple butter

Fill a large stew pan with peeled, quartered, and cored apples. Spice with cloves, allspice, and cinnamon, being careful not to let one spice predominate over the other. Cover with good cider and boil slowly, mashing with a wooden spoon until the whole becomes a dark brown jam, with not more juice remaining than suffices to keep it soft and buttery.

Ginger bread nuts

Dissolve a quarter pound of butter in three quarters of a pound of treacle. Put it into a pan large enough to hold the rest of the ingredients. When almost cold stir in one pound of dried and sifted flour, a quarter pound of coarse brown sugar, three quarter of an ounce of ground ginger, and the peel of a lemon grated. Then mix all these well together. Let it remain till the following day then divide it into pieces the size of a nut. Bake them in buttered tins in a quick oven.

1851

"New-laid eggs should not be used until they have been laid about eight or ten hours, for that part which constitutes the white is not properly set before that time, and does not obtain its delicate flavour."

Portugal cakes

Put in a flat pan one pound of fine sugar and one pound of fresh butter, five eggs and a little mace. Beat all these ingredients together till it is very light and looks curdly. Then put to it one pound of flour and half a pound of currants. Mix well, and then fill small tins and bake them in a slack oven.

Rose water and orange biscuits

Take six eggs, leaving out three whites. Beat them up with two or three spoonfuls of rose or orange flower water. Strew in gradually, half a pound of fine sugar. When the eggs and sugar are thick and white as cream take nine ounces of flour well dried and mix it in. Lay them in long cakes and bake them in a cool oven.

Orange tart

Squeeze, pulp, and boil two Seville oranges tender. Weigh them, and double of sugar. Beat both together to a paste, and then add the juice and pulp of the fruit, and the size of a walnut of fresh butter and beat all together. Choose a very shallow dish, line with a light puff crust and lay the paste of orange in it. Bake. You may ice it.

Sultana cake

One pound of sultanas, a quarter of a pound of moist sugar, one pound of flour, a quarter of a pound of butter, rubbed into the flour, the same weight of candied peel, and two dessert spoonfuls of baking powder. Add half a pint of new milk, lukewarm, and one egg. This cake must be put into the oven immediately.

Plain cake

Three cups of flour, one cup of sugar, one cup of milk, two teaspoonful's of cream of tartar, one teaspoonful of soda, one egg, and a piece of butter the size of an egg. Beat together and bake in oven.

Water cakes

Take three pounds of fine flour, rub it into one pound of sugar sifted, one pound of butter, and one ounce of caraway seed. Make it into a paste with three quarters of a pint of boiling new milk, roll very thin and cut into the size you choose. Punch full of holes, and bake on tin plates in a cool oven.

Small plum cakes

Take one pound of flour, well dried, a little mace, half pound of butter rubbed into the flour, a quarter pound of loaf sugar pounded and sifted, half a pound of currants. Mix these ingredients together with three eggs, well whisked. Put on buttered tins in small lumps, and bake in a moderate oven for a quarter of an hour.

Tea biscuit

One quart of milk, a quarter pound of butter, one half teacup of sugar. Make a sponge. When light, make stiff enough to roll easily. Rise in pans and bake.

German pancake

Beat half a pound of butter to a cream. Mix with it half a pound of flour, half a pound of sugar, twelve egg yolks and a pint of lukewarm cream. Beat the whites of the eggs, and add them together with a little powdered cinnamon and lemon-peel cut thin and chopped very fine. The pancakes are to be done on one side only and placed in a pile, one over the other, so as to form a cake, sugar and cinnamon being strewn between each. The pile is to be cut downwards like a cake and served with wine or jelly sauce.

1856

"Flour should not be kept in the sack, but emptied into a barrel, kept in a dry place, and covered from the dust."

Almond icing

Blanch one pound of sweet almonds and pound them (a few at a time) in a mortar to a paste, adding a little rose water to facilitate the operation. Whisk the whites of four eggs to a strong froth. Mix them with the pounded almonds and stir in sugar. Beat all together. When the cake is sufficiently done lay on the almond icing, and put it into the oven to dry. Before laying this preparation on the cake, great care must be taken that it is nice and smooth, which is easily accomplished by well beating the mixture.

Norfolk biscuits

Take three quarters of a pound of butter, three pounds and a half of flour, and a quarter of a pint of yeast. Melt the butter with water, knead well till stiff, and bake on buttered paper for twenty minutes, an ounce for each biscuit.

Cream meringues

Four eggs (the whites only) whipped stiff, with one pound of powder sugar Add lemon or vanilla for flavour. When very stiff, spoon in the shape of an egg upon stiff letter-paper lining the bottom of your baking pan, putting them half an inch apart. Do not shut the oven door closely, but leave a space so you can watch them. When they are light yellow brown, take them out and cool quickly. Slip a thin bladed knife under each. Scoop out the soft inside, and fill with cream whipped as for Charlotte Ruse. They are very fine. The oven should be very hot.

Rich cherry and almond cake

Mix two pounds of flour, two and a half pounds of butter, three pounds cherries, half pound of fine chopped almonds, one and a half pounds of loaf sugar (ground and sifted). Add a quarter ounce each of mace, ground cloves, nutmeg and cinnamon. To sixteen egg yolks and half of the whites, add half a quart of sack and the same of brandy. Mix all together. Add half a pound of citron or orange peel minced. Bake in oven till done.

Gingerbread cake

One pound flour, three quarters of a pound of butter, three quarters of a pound grated loaf sugar, half a pound of orange peel, two ounces ground ginger, one ounce ground cinnamon, half an ounce of ground cloves, two nutmegs grated, one dozen white peppercorns ground, ten eggs, one pound of treacle. Fresh butter is best, but if salted let it be well washed and then worked with a cream. The yolks and whites of the eggs to be beaten separately; the former longer than the latter and until it becomes like cream, then mix both together and add them by decrees to the butter, working it well till thoroughly incorporated. Let all the dry ingredients be mixed together, and added by degrees to the butter and eggs. When about a third part of these are in, add the treacle and work the whole well for five or six minutes. A little soda makes the cake lighter. It takes an hour and three-quarters of rather a brisk fire.

Puff paste (pastry) with brandy

Take one pound of dry, sifted flour, and the same quantity of butter. Divide the flour in two, and put one half on the pastry board. Make a hollow in the centre of it, and pour in three eggs with a glass of brandy. Make it up into a lump, and lay it aside. Take the butter and roll it out in the other half of the flour, then take the lump, roll it out thin, and lay in the butter in five portions. Always roll the pastry one way, and away from you. Let the pastry be all night in a cool place, and it will be fit to use in the morning.

1853

"What a variety of culinary modes prevail at the diggings. Here is a scion of a distinguished English family, superintending at a slow fire the frizzling of his mutton chops on a grid iron, formed on an iron hoop bent in and out and turning his chops with little tongs of the same material. He lets no gravy escape. He is an epicurean poor fellow, rather down in the world. But richer than his neighbour, who has neither camp oven, pan, nor grid iron – nothing except a tin billy in which he boils his meat, suet dumplings and makes his soup, his tea and his coffee."

Victoria sandwiches

Cut sponge cake into slices a quarter of an inch thick, spread some apricot jam, or other preserve. On the top of one slice, cover with another, press down gently, and cut into large diamonds. Cover with pink icing, and put in an oven to set.

Light sponge cake

To three quarters of a pound of lump sugar put a teacupful of boiling water. Set it on the fire, and make it boil. Then pour it hot over six eggs. Whisk them together for half an hour then add eight ounces of flour and the minced peel of one lemon. Mix them all together, and bake three quarters of an hour.

Gingerbread

Mix two and a half pounds of flour with half a pound of butter, the rind of a lemon grated, four ounces of moist sugar, and half an ounce of pounded ginger. Make this into a pastry with one pound of warm treacle. Lay it in cakes on a tea plate and bake.

Puddings & pancakes

Light paste (pastry) for tarts and cheesecakes

Beat the white of an egg to a stiff froth, then mix with as much water as will make three quarters of a pound of flour into a very stiff pastry. Take a half a pound of butter and cut it into thirds. Roll it very thin then lay one third of the butter upon it in little bits. Dredge it with some flour and roll it up tight. Roll it out again and put another of butter. Repeat till it all be worked up.

Iced hamburgh pudding

The peel of a lemon, one pint rich cream, a little mace and sugar to taste, to be boiled a quarter of an hour. Then take out the lemon peel, beat it in a mortar, force it through a sieve, mix it with a little cream. Have ready the yolks of eight eggs well beaten. Stir it all together, put it in a mould, and boil for twenty minutes. Add a few almonds to flavour it. This should be made the night before it is required, and the next morning put into ice, and turned out just before it is sent to table.

Prune tart

Give prunes a scald, take out the stones, and break them apart. Put the kernels into a little cranberry juice, with the prunes and sugar. Simmer, and when cold make into a pastry tart.

Potato balls

Boil the potatoes then carefully wash them. Boil a pint of milk, with some lemon peel, a little sugar, and salt. When the milk boils add the potatoes, so as to form a tolerably thick mash. When cold make it into balls, cover them with bread crumbs and the yolk of egg. Fry till a nice brown colour, and serve with sugar strewed over them.

Soufflé pudding

Take a slice of bread and crumble it into a dish. Whisk the yolks of seven eggs, and mix them with some milk. Lay some fruit preserve in a dish, pour in the mixture, and fire in an oven for half an hour or three-quarters, then take it out and let it cool. Beat the whites of the eggs to a froth, mix them with pounded white sugar and lay this on the top. Put it in the oven again until the whites become slightly brown. Sweeten to taste. Sponge cake will do instead of bread.

Orange pudding

Peel and cut five good sweet, juicy oranges into thin slices, taking out all the seeds. Pour over them a coffee cup of white sugar. Let a pint of milk get boiling hot by setting it into some boiling water; add the yolk of three eggs well beaten, one tablespoonful of corn starch made smooth with a little cold milk. Stir all the time, and as soon as thickened pour it over the fruit. Beat the whites to a stiff froth adding a tablespoonful of sugar, and spread over the top for frosting. Set it into the oven for a few minutes to harden. Best cold or hot for dinner or tea. Substitute berries of any kind, or peaches if you like them better than oranges.

Potato fritters

Boil and beat half a dozen potatoes, mix with four beaten eggs, about a gill of cream, some salt and nutmeg, a little sugar, some fresh butter oiled and a tablespoonful of spirits. Beat well together, drop in the boiling dripping and until a light brown. Serve hot with strewn sugar over them.

1882

"Selecting flour - look at its colour – if it is white with a straw coloured tint it is good. If it has flecks it is not good. Squeeze some of the flour in your hand. If it retains the shape given it by pressure it is a good sign. When kneaded it is very ductile, partaking of an elastic and glutinous nature, is easy to work up, and being adhesive, can be squeezed, elongated, or drawn out, without breaking. Bad flour of course has opposite qualities."

Quick pudding

Warm one pint of milk, stir in a quarter of a pound of butter, and let it cool before the other ingredients are added to it. Stir in half a pound of sifted sugar, one quarter of a pound of flour, and five egg yolks and three egg whites which should be well whisked. Flavour with a little grated lemon rind, and beat the mixture well. Butter some small cups, rather more than half fill them, bake from twenty minutes to half an hour, according to the size of the puddings and serve with fruit, custard, or wine sauce a little of which may be poured over them.

Dutch curd pudding

Beat half a pound of curd and half a pound of butter to a cream. Whip into it seven well beaten eggs, a quarter pound of sugar, the same of washed currants, half a lemon grated, and half a nutmeg grated. Beat it to the moment of baking. Sift sugar over.

Christmas plum pudding

Stone and cut one and a half pounds of raisins in halves, but do not chop them. Wash and dry a half pound of currants and mince three quarters of a pound of suet very finely. Cut half a pound of mixed peel into thin slices and grate half a pound of bread. When these ingredients are prepared, mix them well together then moisten the mixture with eight well beaten eggs. Add a wine-glassful of brandy. Stir well so that everything may be thoroughly blended, and press the pudding into a buttered mould. Tie it down tightly, and boil it five or six hours. It may be boiled in a cloth without a mould, and will require the same time for cooking.

As Christmas puddings are usually made a few days before they are required for table, when the pudding is taken out of the pot, hang it up immediately, and put a plate or saucer underneath to catch the matter that may drain from it. The day it is to be eaten plunge it into boiling water and keep it boiling for at least two hours, then turn it out of the mould and serve it with brandy sauce. On Christmas day a sprig of holly is usually placed in the middle of the pudding, and about a wine-glass of brandy poured round it, which, at the moment of serving, is lighted, and the pudding thus brought to table encircled in flame.

 1886

"The custom of placing an inverted cup in a fruit pie is to contain the juice while the pie is cooking. When the cup is first put into the dish it is full of cold air. When heated it will condense and draw up the juice thus preventing it from boiling over. If a glass tumbler is inverted in the pie, its contents can be examined while it is in the oven."

Excellent potato pudding

Take eight ounces of boiled potatoes, two ounces of butter, the yolks and whites of three eggs, a quarter of a pint of cream, one spoonful of white wine, a morsel of salt and rind of a lemon. Beat all to a froth, sugar to taste. A crust or not as you like. Bake it in a moderate oven.

Quaking pudding

Scald a quart of cream. When almost cold put to it four well beaten eggs, a spoonful of flour, some nutmeg and sugar. Tie it close in a buttered cloth. Boil it for an hour. Turn it out with care lest it should crack. Serve with melted butter, a little wine and sugar. To make a lighter and fluffier pudding use five eggs and a little less cream.

Ground rice pudding

Boil a large spoonful heaped of ground rice in a pint of new milk with lemon peel and cinnamon. When cold add sugar, nutmeg, and two eggs well beaten.

Muscatel plum pudding

Stone and cut one and a half pounds of Muscatel raisins, wash and dry one and three quarter pounds of currants and one pound of sultana raisins. Cut six ounces of mixed candied peel in thin slices. Grate two pounds of bread crumbs and chop two pounds of suet very fine. Flavour with the rind of two lemons, one ounce of ground nutmeg, one ounce of ground cinnamon, and one ounce of pounded almonds. Mix all the dry ingredients well together, and moisten with sixteen well beaten and strained eggs. Stir in a quarter pint of brandy and thoroughly mix. Well butter and flour a stout new pudding cloth. Put in the pudding and tie it down very tightly and closely. Boil from six to eight hours. Serve with brandy sauce. This quantity may be divided and boiled in buttered moulds. For small families this is the most desirable way, as the above will be found to make a pudding of rather, large dimensions.

Baked cheesecake

Strain the whey from the curd of two quarts of milk. When rather dry crumble the curd through a coarse sieve and mix with two ounces of butter, one ounce of pounded almonds, a little orange flower water, half a glass of raisin wine, a grated biscuit, four ounces of currants, some nutmeg and powdered cinnamon. Beat all the above with three eggs and half a pint of cream, till quite light. Then fill patty-pans three parts full. Bake in oven.

Small potato cheesecakes

Boil six ounces of potatoes and four ounces of lemon peel. Beat the latter in a marble mortar with four ounces of sugar, then add the potatoes beaten and four ounces of butter melted in a little cream. When well mixed let it stand for half an hour. Line patty pans with pastry and rather more than half fill them with the mixture. Bake in quick oven for half an hour, sifting some double refined sugar on them when going to the oven. This quantity will make a dozen.

Apple snow

Peel, core, and cut ten good sized apples into quarters. Put into a lined saucepan with the rind of a lemon and sufficient water to prevent them from burning, rather less than half a pint. When they are tender, take out the peel and beat the apples to a pulp. Let them cool, and stir in the whites of ten eggs, which should be previously beaten to a strong froth. Add half a pound of pounded sugar, continue the whisking until the mixture becomes quite stiff. The either heap it on a glass dish or serve it in small glasses. The dish may be garnished with preserved barberries or strips of bright coloured jelly, and a dish of custards should be served with it, or a jug of cream.

Cream pancakes

Mix the yolks of two well beaten eggs with a pint of cream. Add two ounces of sifted sugar, a little nutmeg, cinnamon and mace. Rub the pan with butter, and fry the pancakes thin.

1853

"In the next tent, the steaks have been fried and the cook is just pouring over the hissing fat a pannikin of flour and cold water blended to make a pancake, a veritable pancake without eggs. And right pleasant to the taste. Ay, he can present you with a splendid plum pudding without plums or eggs, butter nor spices. Think of that and blush, ye extravagant English dames."

Irish pancakes

Beat eight yolks and five egg whites and then strain them into a pint of cream. Warm this mixture. Put in grated nutmeg and sugar to taste. Set three ounces of fresh butter on the fire, stir it, and as it warms pour in the cream. Then add almost a half a pound of flour. Mix until smooth. Fry the pancake very thin, the first with a bit of butter but not the others. Serve several on one another.

Rice pancakes

Boil half a pound of rice in a small quantity of water until it jellies. When cold, mix it with a pint of cream, eight eggs, a bit of salt, and nutmeg. Stir in eight ounces of butter first warmed, and add as much flour as will make the batter thick enough. Fry in as little butter or lard as possible.

Arrowroot pudding

Mix a dessertspoonful of Arrowroot powder in two of cold milk. Pour upon it a pint of boiling milk in which has been dissolved four ounces of butter and two of sugar, stirring all the time. Add a little nutmeg and five eggs. Bake half hour in a dish lined with pastry. Preserved fruit, of any kind, laid at the bottom eats well. If to look clear, substitute water for milk.

Eve's pudding

Grate three quarters of a pound of bread. Mix it with the same quantity of shredded suet, the same of apples and also of currants. Mix with these the whole of four eggs, and the rind of half a lemon finely shredded. Put it into a mould and boil for three hours. Serve with pudding sauce, the juice of half a lemon, and a little nutmeg.

1858

An effort to protect the oyster population saw the harvesting of oysters in Victoria illegal during the summer months. The fine for being caught with Oysters from October to January was £10

Baked tapioca pudding

One teacup of tapioca, one quart of milk. Soak the tapioca an hour or two in the milk. Add four eggs and a little butter and salt. Sweeten and flavour to your taste. Pour in pan and bake until done.

German puddings or puffs

Melt three ounces of butter in a pint of cream. Let it stand till nearly cold. Then mix two ounces of flour and two ounces sugar, four egg yolks and two egg whites, and a little rose or orange flower water. Bake in little cups, buttered, half an hour. They should be served the moment they are done, or they will not be light. Turn out of the cups and serve with white wine and sugar.

Coconut pudding

Over a low heat melt together two ounces of fresh butter and four ounces of pounded sugar. Then boil for ten minutes. Add two ounces of finely grated coconut, one ounce of finely chopped citron. Add four eggs and the grated rind of a large lemon. When these ingredients have been well beaten together, add the strained juice of half a lemon, then put the mixture into a mould. Bake in a moderate oven for three quarters of an hour.

Chocolate pie

Beat an egg to a stiff froth, then add pulverised sugar and grated chocolate, with a half teaspoonful of vanilla. Spread this on top of the pie and let it harden for a moment in the oven. Or you may prepare it still another way. Put the chocolate in a basin on the back of the stove and let it melt (do not put a drop of water with it). When melted, beat the one egg and some sugar in with it - in the latter case it will be regular choco-brown in colour, and in the other a sort of grey.

Raised doughnuts

One pint of milk, one pint of sugar, yeast, one half pint of lard, two eggs, one spoonful of salt, one teaspoonful of soda, dissolved in a teacup of water - flour to roll out. Mix well and leave to rise. Bake.

Minute pudding

Place over the fire one teacup of sweet milk for each person, let it come to a boil. Stir in one egg, one tablespoonful of flour and then set with a little milk. Stir it well, let it cook a few minutes. Butter common teacups and put the pudding into them. When cool, the pudding will slip out. Serve with sweet cream or preserve.

Apple puffs

Pare and core the fruit and either stove them in a stone jar on a hot hearth, or bake them. When cold, mix the pulp of the apple with sugar and finely shredded lemon, a small glass of wine and a little brandy. Give the whole one scald, and put in cups to be eaten cold.

Biscuit pudding

Slice four common biscuits thin. Boil them in three gills of new milk, with a piece of lemon peel shredded as fine as possible. Break it to a mash, to which put three ounces of warmed butter, two ounces of sugar, and four eggs well beaten. Add a large spoonful of brandy. Bake or boil.

1887

"Don't make tea in a tin pot. The tannin, which is acid, attacks the tin and produces a poison. Don't use water which has stood in a load pipe over the night. Not less than a bucketful should be allowed to run."

Spanish fritters

Cut the crumb of a French roll into lengths as thick as finger, in what shape you please. Soak in some cream, nutmeg, sugar, grounded cinnamon, and a beaten egg. When well soaked fry to a nice brown, and serve with butter, wine and sweet sauce.

Pink fritters

Boil a large beetroot until tender then beat it fine in marble mortar. Add the yolk of four eggs, two spoonfuls of flour, and three of cream. Add the juice and peel of half a lemon, half a grated nutmeg, and a glass of brandy. Mix all together, and fry the fritters in butter. Garnish them with preserved apricots or sprigs of myrtle.

Curd fritters

Rub down in a mortar a quart of dried curd and with the yolks of eight and whites of four well-beaten eggs. A two ounces of sifted sugar, half a grated nutmeg, and half a spoonful of flour. Drop the batter into frying-pan with a little butter or fine lard.

Oatmeal pudding

Pour a quart of boiling milk over a pint of the best fine oatmeal. Let it soak all night. The next day beat two eggs and mix with a little salt. Add the oatmeal and pour into a buttered basin that will just hold it. Cover it tight with a floured cloth, and boil it an hour and a half. Eat it with cold butter and salt. When cold slice and toast it, and eat it as oat-cake buttered.

1872

"When cows are fed on turnips, their milk is apt to taste of that vegetable. This may be prevented by putting a small quantity of saltpetre into the pail into which the cow is milked."

Potato fritters

Slice potatoes thin. Make a batter of flour, water, lemon peel and a spoonful of orange flower water. Dip the potato slices in the batter and fry in butter. Serve with white sugar sifted over them.

Shelford pudding

Mix three quarters of a pound of currants or raisins, one pound of suet, one pound of flour, six eggs a little good milk, some lemon-peel and a little salt. Boil in a melon shaped bowl for six hours.

Royal fritters

Put one pint of sweet milk into a saucepan over the fire, and as soon as it commences to boil pour in one half pint of white wine and let it stand for a few minutes to cool. Skim off the curd and put it into a basin. Add one ounce of powdered sugar, a little grated lemon rind and three eggs well whisked. Beat the whole well together, adding sufficient flour to make a smooth, stiff batter, and fry the fritters quickly in plenty of hot lard until they are browned. Then drain them on a sieve and serve on a hot dish.

Brown bread pudding

Take half a pound of stale brown bread grated, ditto of currants, ditto of shredded suet and sugar. Add nutmeg mixed with four eggs, a spoonful of brandy and two tablespoons of cream. Boil in a basin that exactly holds it for three or four hours. Serve with sweet sauce.

Marrow pudding

Grate a penny loaf into crumbs and pour on it a pint of boiling cream or milk. Cut very thin a pound of beef marrow. Beat four eggs well, add a wineglass of brandy or sherry, with sugar and nutmeg to taste. Mix all well together, and wither boil or bake for three quarters of an hour. Cut two ounces of candied citron thin, and scatter over the top when serving.

Sponge pudding

Break some stale sponge cakes into a buttered mould, strew amongst them chips of candied peel. Fill the mould rather more than half full. Make a good custard, with a glass of brandy in it. Pour it into the mould and let it stand for an hour. Steam the pudding for an hour and a half. Dissolve some red currant jelly in a very little warm water; when the pudding is dished pour the jelly over it, and serve with arrowroot and brandy sauce.

Apple cheese

Boil some large green baking apples in a quantity of water until the skin begins to crack, then drain off the water and let the apples cool. When cold take off the skin and rub the pulp from the core. Blend it smooth and to every pound of pulp add a pound of white sugar, the rind of a lemon, grated, and half the juice. Boil all together till the fruit looks clear. Put it into china shapes. It will turn out quite stiff and make a nice supper dish. If intended to be kept for some time cover close like jam.

Coffee ice pudding

Pound two ounces of freshly roasted coffee in a mortar, just enough to crush the berries without reducing them to powder. Put them into a pint of milk with half a pound of loaf sugar. Let it boil then leave it to get cold. Strain it on the yolks of six eggs in a double saucepan, and stir it on the fire till the custard thickens. When quite cold work into it a gill and a half of cream whipped to a froth. Freeze the mixture.

Suet pudding

Three ounces of flour, ditto of finely grated bread-crumbs and six of beef suet chopped fine, six of raisins weighed after being stoned, ditto well cleaned currants, four ounces of minced apples and citron, five of sugar, two of candied orange peel, half a teaspoon of nutmeg and powdered mace, a little salt, a glass of old brandy and three eggs. Mix and beat these ingredients together. Tie them tightly in a thickly floured cloth, and boil for three hours and a half.

Jams, jellies & sherbets

Damson jelly

Put the damson fruit in a jar in the oven to drain out the juice. To every pint of juice put three quarters of a pound of lump sugar and boil it half-an-hour. When it is quite clear pour it into moulds.

Black cherry preserve

Boil the cherries in sugar and water until they are reduced to a pulp. Then add more cherries, and half their weight of loaf-sugar, and continue to boil them until they become of the proper consistence.

Melon jam

Scrape the skin off the melon, throw away the pulp and the seeds (or sow them). Cut the melon in strips and put the whole in a pan. Throw sugar all over it in the same weight as the melon. Let it stand thus for ten to twelve hours when sufficient juice will be found to boil it. Cook for about one hour and flavour to taste. It is advisable to add some brandy to prevent fermentation in hot weather – say a half pint to the gallon. It can be flavoured with orange, lemon, cinnamon etc.

Quince jelly

Pare, core, and quarter some ripe but perfectly sound quinces as quickly as possible, and throw them as they are done into part of the water into which they are to be boiled. Allow one pint of this to each pound of fruit, and simmer it gently until it is a little broken, but not so long as to redden the juice, which ought to be very pale. Turn the whole into a jelly bag, and let it drain very closely from it, but without the slightest pressure. Weigh the juice, put it into a preserving pan and boil it quickly for twenty minutes. Take it from the fire and stir in it until it is entirely dissolved, twelve ounces of sugar to each pound of juice, or fourteen should the fruit be very acid. Keep it constantly stirred and cleared from scum from ten to twenty minutes longer, or until it jellies strongly in falling from the skimmer. Turn into moulds. If properly made it will turn out firm and transparent. Note, to each pound of quince one pint of water, to each pound of juice twelve ounces of sugar.

Strawberry and raspberry acid

Dissolve two and a half ounces of tartaric acid in a quart of spring water, pour it over five pounds of fruit, let it stand for a day, taking care not to bruise the fruit. Then take it up carefully with a saucer, and strain it through a fine sieve. To every pint add one and a half pounds of finely powdered sugar, stir it frequently, and when quite dissolved and all the scum off put it in bottles. The whole process must be cold. By adding an ounce of isinglass dissolved and strained to the pint of syrup it will make a pretty mould of jelly. Carbonate of soda with water added to this acid makes a pleasant effervescing drink.

Apple jelly

Pare, core, and stew six eight apples with lemon peel, sugar, and sufficient water to cover them. Add half an ounce of gelatine. Dip a mould in cold water, pour in, and when cold, turn it out.

Plum preserve

Set a pint of water and a pound of sugar on the fire, and put the plums in an earthen basin. When the syrup boils pour it on the plums, and let them stand all night. In the morning boil them till they are tender, then put them in jars. If need be, boil the syrup longer till it will rope, then let it be cold, and pour it on the plums.

Black currant sherbet

Gather the currants when quite ripe, pick them off the stalks, and put them in a stone jar, with a quart of water to five quarts of currants. Tie the jar down close with double paper, and set it in a cool oven for two or three hours, or it may be put in a kettle of cold water, which is then to be very gradually heated but not to the boiling point. When the currants are sufficiently soft, squeeze the whole through a thin bag. Add to each quart of the juice, the juice of a large lemon and a pound and a quarter of loaf sugar. When the sugar is melted, finish as red currant sherbet.

Jelly for cakes

One cup of sugar, one lemon – grate the rind and squeeze out the juice - one egg, one tablespoonful of butter. Beat altogether, and let it boil.

Currant and raspberry sherbet

Press the juice from ripe red currants, mix with a pint and half of juice from raspberries (or melted raspberry jelly) and a pint of water. Strain it clear and dissolve in it one pound and a half of the best loaf sugar. When the sugar is all dissolved, pour it into a bowl, and freeze in the same way as ice-cream. It will not require a second freezing, but may he served in glasses as soon as frozen. The raspberry juice may be omitted, but it is an improvement.

1872

"To carve standing is considered vulgar."

Bottled raspberry preserve

Take an equal quantity of crushed fruit and powdered loaf sugar, mix well together, and put them into wine bottles, cork tight and resin the corks. In this way of preserving without boiling, the colour and flavour are very fine, and they will keep through the year.

Cherry sherbet

Red juicy cherries are best. Stone them, and squeeze through a bag. A pound and half of loaf sugar to a quart of juice will be enough. Black cherries do not require so much. A little raspberry juice is an improvement to the red cherry, and red currant juice to the black cherry. Half a pint of water to a quart of cherry juice is sufficient, as sherry sherbet should be rich, but a pint or even a larger proportion of water is commonly used with any kind of fruit. Put the sugar, broken into small lumps, into a preserving kettle, pour on the quantity of water you intend using, and stir it until the sugar is all dissolved. Then boil and skim it quite clear, after which it is to be stirred into the juice of the fruit. The kernels of cherries, plums, or similar fruits, may be boiled in the syrup.

Rhubarb preserve

A preserve, applicable to winter use in almost every kind of way, and, when well made, ornamental and elegant in appearance, may be made from their stalks, and be called rhubarb jam, or rhubarb marmalade. After the skin and fibre are removed, equal weights of good brown sugar and of the stalks so prepared (and cut in small pieces) are to be taken. After the sugar has been boiled pretty thick and well skimmed (half a pint of water being allowed to every three pounds), the rhubarb, with a few pieces of ginger, is to be added and the whole boiled till it falls and till the preserve looks clear. This preserve will keep for years. If the small kinds of scarlet are used, the skin and fibres may be left in, and the pieces cut much smaller than with the other sorts. This will give a beautiful colour.

Blackberry jam

To every pound of fruit add half a pound of coarse moist sugar, and boil for three quarters of an hour. A wooden spoon should be used for stirring it, as iron spoils the colour. This is a plain, homely method, so cheap and easily managed as to be practicable in every cottage. There is no fruit more salutary for children than blackberries.

Cherry jam

To twelve pounds of ripe Kentish or Duke Cherries, weigh one pound of sugar. Break the stones of part and blanch them, then put them to the fruit and sugar and boil all gently, till the jam comes clear from the pan. Pour it into china plates to come up dry to table.

94

Custards & sauces

Lemon cream

Beat the whites of nine eggs and the yolk of one well with six tablespoonfuls of water. Put in the juice of four lemons with the peel of one and beat it all together. Sugar to your taste. Strain it and set it on the fire, stirring all the time till it is clear and as thick as cream.

Spanish sherbet

Take full grown grapes before they begin to ripen, and having picked and washed them, put them into a wooden bowl and mash them well to get as much juice as possible. Mix it with half the quantity of water and sugar to sweeten it. The run it through a flannel jelly bag several times, till it is perfectly clear and bright, then freeze as usual. A pound and a quarter of sugar to a quart of grape juice is about the right quantity.

Almond custard

Blanch and beat four ounces of almonds fine, with a spoonful of water. Beat a pint of cream with two spoonfuls of rose-water, and put them to the yolks of four eggs and as much sugar as will make it pretty sweet. Then add the almonds. Stir it over a slow fire till it is of a proper thickness, but do not boil. Pour it into custard glasses.

Seville orange custard

Boil until very tender the rind of half a Seville orange then beat it in a mortar to a paste. Put in a spoonful of the very best brandy, the juice of a Seville orange, four ounces of lump sugar, and the well beaten yolks of four eggs. Beat all together for ten minutes and pour in by degrees a pint of boiling cream. Keep beating until the mixture is cold, then put into custard cups. Set them in a dish of boiling water and let them stand until thick. Then put preserved orange peel in slices upon the custard. Serve either hot or cold.

Ornamented custard pudding

Put a rich custard into a shallow dish. When it shall have become cold lay on it, in any shape you please, the beaten whites of two new laid eggs in a firm froth, and over that sift refined sugar. Put it into an oven to become a fine light brown.

Thick vanilla cream

Boil half a stick of vanilla in a quarter of a pint of new milk until it has a very high flavour. Have ready a jelly made of an ounce of isinglass to a pint of water. Mix with the milk and a pint and a quarter of fine cream. Sweeten with fine sugar and stir till nearly cold. Then dip a mould into cold water and pour the whole into it. Make it the day before it be wanted.

Wine or brandy sauce

Cut a quarter pound of butter into small pieces, put it into the saucepan. Dredge over a dessertspoonful of flour and add two wine-glassfuls of water. Stir it one way constantly till the whole of the ingredients are melted and thoroughly blended, then stir in three heaped teaspoonful of pounded sugar, and a large wine-glassful of port or sherry, or a small one of brandy. Bring the sauce to the point of boiling. Serve in a boat or tureen separately. To convert this into punch sauce add to the sherry and brandy a small wine-glassful of rum, and the juice and grated rind of a lemon. Liqueurs such as maraschino or curacoa substituted for the brandy make excellent sauce.

Glazing for tarts

Mix sifted sugar and water into a thick paste like cream, and brush it over the crust.

Rice blacmange

Wash a tablespoonful of best rice in two waters, then set it to boil with a small bit of lemon peel or cinnamon, and two tablespoonfuls of white sugar in half a pint of milk. If the rice absorbs all the milk, add as much more as will keep it soft and moist. When boiled to a pulp, put it into a mould till cold, when it will turn out.

American butter sauce

Wash a quarter of a pound of fresh butter with a wooden spoon in two or three waters, to remove every particle of salt. Beat it with the spoon always the same way till it is like cream, then take a whisk and whisk it till quite white, adding to it very gradually two tablespoonfuls of powdered sugar and a glass of sherry, with a little essence of lemon or orange flower water in it. This sauce is extremely nice with puddings.

1886

"Dried fruits ought to be clean and dry, and yet fresh in appearance. When adhering together in lumps they are generally of an inferior quality."

Vanilla cream

Boil a stick of vanilla in a quart of milk, until it has imbibed the perfume. Take it off the fire, and sweeten to your taste, removing the vanilla, which will serve for several times. Break six egg yolks and one whole egg into a bowl. Beat them up and pour in your milk, stirring all the while, to mix them completely. Let it simmer until it is of the consistency of thick boiled custard. Serve in cups or glasses, with a ratafia or small macaroon on the top of each cream.

Devonshire butter

This mode of making Devonshire butter will be useful to the colonist. Scald the cream in a zinc pan, over a charcoal fire, but mind it does not boil. Next morning, when cold, take the cream off. Put it in a wide wooden bowl, and stir it for ten or fifteen minutes, and the butter will come the same as if churned. In the back parts of a settlement, where the farmer has no churn, this hint will be valuable.

Drinks

Barley water

Put half a gallon of water into a very clean saucepan with two ounces of clean (but unwashed) pearl barley. When boiling, carefully skim it with a tablespoon, and add half the rind of a small lemon. Let it boil until the barley is quite tender and sweeten with half an ounce of white sugar. Strain it through a fine sieve.

Currant water

Having strained the juice of currants, red or black, sweeten it to your taste, and fill the glasses about one third, then fill up with ice water. Grate nutmeg over and serve. Or, when the currants are stripped from the stalks, boil a pint of them in a pint of water for ten minutes, then strain and sweeten to taste. Serve warm.

Punch a la romaine

Take five eggs and beat the yolks and whites separately till they will not fall out of a basin; add five tablespoonful's of loaf sugar or a little more, mix them together by degrees, half a tumbler of rum and five ladles of milk by degrees.

Crambambuli punch

Take two bottles of light ale and boil in a pan. Then put into the liquor half a pint of rum, and from half a pound to a pound of loaf sugar. After this has been boiled for a few minutes, take the whole from the fire, and put into the mixture the whites and the yolks of from six to eight eggs, previously well whisked. Stir the whole for a minute or two, and pour it to a punch bowl, to be drunk out of tumblers. It tastes well hot or cold.

King cup

Squeeze the juice of a lemon into a china bowl, add the rind cut very thin, an ounce of white sugar, a good sized piece of bruised ginger. Pour over them a pint and a half of boiling water. Let it stand till cold, then strain. Add two glasses of sherry, and ice it with lumps of clear ice.

Bitter Ale

To make 100 gallons, use nine bushels of malt, or ten if strength is desired, twenty three or twenty seven of Kentish hops, according to the required degree of bitterness. Take three pounds of camomile flowers, stewed in a jar and strained. Boil the malt and water till the liquor begins to fine itself, and that is the time to add the hops and flowers. Put the camomile flowers and hops in at the same time.

Ginger beer

Take ten gallons of water and when boiling add ten pounds of sugar. Skim well for ten minutes. Have ready one pound of ginger which has been previously soaked in boiling water. Put the ginger in a cask and pour the boiling liquor on it. Then put in one half pound of cream of tartare into a jug and fill with boiling water. When the liquor in the cask becomes lukewarm, add it, keeping the whole well stirred. Then take the white of four eggs well beaten and work them into the cask. Add a small quantity of lemon juice to taste. Bottle in twenty four hours in stone bottles and tie down. It will keep good for a month or longer.

Veal sherbet

Wash a good knuckle of veal, and put it to boil in nine pints of water. Let it boil until reduced to two pints. Run it through a fine sieve, and when nearly cold, add to it two pints of clarified syrup, and a pint and a half of clear lemon juice. Mix well and serve as refreshment.

Lemon sherbet

Put into a large bowl one pound of loaf sugar and the juice and rinds of three lemons. Pour over them a quart of boiling water, and let them stand all night. Next day, strain the liquor through a cloth. Add to it five bottles of currant wine. Mix all well together, and bottle off for use. When wanted, mix with cold spring water in a tumbler.

Orangeade

Squeeze out the juice of an orange. Pour boiling water on a little of the peel, and cover it close. Boil water and sugar to a thin syrup, and skin it. When all are cold, mix the juice, the infusion, and the syrup with as much more water as will make a rich drink. Strain through a jelly-bag and ice.

Apple cider

As soon as the apples are ripe collect them in heaps on the grass. By no means house them, or the cider will be musty. After they are ground and pressed pass the liquid through a flannel bag to strain off any bits of skin or core that may have adhered to the cloths. Put it at once into casks; do not touch it until it has done fermenting; then put in the bungs.

Raisin wine

Allow one gallon of water to every six pounds of chopped raisins. First put half that quantity of water to the fruit, and let it stand for ten days, stirring it every day, then strain it off. Then put the other half of the water to the raisins, and let it stand another ten days. Strain it off, and mix the two liquors together. Yon will have to draw off the wine two or three times before it is fit to bottle.

Rhubarb wine

Take as many rhubarb stalks as you think you may require, (you may make more wine next week if the quantity is not sufficient), peel and bruise them, and pour cold spring water on them, in the proportion of an imperial quart to a pound. Stir the mash twice a day for three days, then press and strain, adding sugar in the proportion of two and one half pounds per gallon, and brandy according to taste. Barrel it, suspending a linen bag of isinglass in the centre of each barrel. It must be stopped very close, and in from six to nine months according to temperature, it will be ready to be bottled off for use. All the kinds of rhubarb will answer for this purpose.

Around the home

For hoarseness

For a sore throat and hoarseness, heat up some mutton suet and molasses together. Take a teaspoonful occasionally. Wearing a suet plaster on the throat and breast may also be regarded as a remedy. Afflicted ones try it.

Chest colds

A piece of flannel, dipped in brandy, and applied to the chest, and covered with dry flannel, is to be worn all night. Four or six small onions, boiled, and put on buttered toast, and eaten for supper, is likewise good for colds on the chest.

Toothache

Roasted onions applied to the wrist will relieve the toothache.

Common cough

Slice a common turnip rather thin and sprinkle brown sugar over it. Let it stand for a few hours with a saucer pressed down on it, and the syrup which runs from it will be found very soothing to the chest if sipped frequently.

Toilet vinegar

Half a pint of the best white wine vinegar, half a pint of pale rum; essence of bergamot rosemary, and marjoram, (a drachm each) and one pint of rose or elder flower water. Mix the perfumes with the spirit, then add the vinegar, and lastly, the rose water. If not perfectly bright it may be strained through blotting paper.

Antidote for poison ivy, insect bites

A standing antidote for poison oak, ivy, etc., is to take a handful of quick lime, dissolve in water, let it stand half an hour, then paint the poisoned part with it. Three to four applications will never fail to cure the most aggravated cases. Poison from bees, hornets, spider bites, etc. is instantly arrested by the application equal parts of common salt and bicarbonate of soda well rubbed in on the places bitten or stung.

Cure for corns

Soak some young ivy leaves in vinegar for a few hours, then tie one of the leaves on the corn. It should be changed each night and morning, and in a few days the corn can be taken out without any pain. The leaves should be continued a day or two after the corn has been taken out, in order to remove any little hardness that may remain.

Relief for asthma

Two ounces of the best honey and one ounce of castor oil mixed. A teaspoonful to be taken night and morning.

Mustard whey

Boil four drachma of the bruised seeds of mustard in a pint of milk, then strain and separate the curd. A fourth part should be taken three times a day.

Homemade soap

The following makes family soap at about a penny per pound. Take ten quarts of water, add to this six pounds of quick lime - shell lime is the best - and six pounds common washing soda. Put all together, and boil for half an hour, then let it stand all night to clear. Draw off the ley, and add to it one pound of common resin and seven pounds of fat - any fat will do. Boil this for half an hour, then let it stand till cool and cut into bars.

Hair wash

Drop a lump of fresh quick lime the size of a walnut into a pint of water, and allow it to stand all night. Mix the water, after being poured off from the sediment, with a quarter of a pint of the best vinegar. It is to be applied to the roots of the hair.

A useful lotion

The blooms of the common marigold (calendula), infused in equal parts of pure alcohol and water, is an admirable remedy for all kind of wounds, cuts, bruises, and burns, on man or beast. Its effect in allaying pain and removing soreness is similar to that of tincture of arnica. One ounce of the blooms to a half-pint of alcohol and a half-pint water is the recipe.

Keeping flowers

As you are fond of having flowers in the room, you will perhaps be glad to know how to preserve cut flowers as long as possible. The most simple rules are, not to put too many flowers into one glass, to change the water every morning, and remove every decayed leaf as soon as it appears, cutting off the ends of the stems occasionally, as soon as they show any symptoms of decay. A more efficacious way, however, is to put nitrate of soda into the water. About as much as can be easily taken up between the forefinger and thumb, put into the glass every time the water is changed, will preserve cut flowers in all their beauty for above a fortnight. Nitrate of potash (that is, common saltpetre), in powder, has nearly the same effect, but is hot quite so efficacious.

To renovate black silk

Slice some uncooked potatoes, pour boiling water on them. When cold sponge the right side of the silk with it, and iron it on the wrong.

To preserve geraniums during winter

Take the plants out of the pots, trim off the leaves and outer branches, take all the soil from the roots, tie the plants in bunches, and hang them roots upwards, in a dry, dark cupboard, loft, or cellar, where no frost can touch them. In spring re-pot them in a good compost, first carefully cleansing the pots within and without.

Waterproof for leather boots

Take half a pint of linseed oil and half a pint of neatsfoot oil, and boil them together. When the boots to be waterproofed are dry and free from dirt, rub them well with this mixture before the fire until completely saturated. Set them by for two or three days after oiling the first time, and after using, wash them clean from dirt and oil when dry, or upon the feet before going out.

To wash flannels

Put the flannel into a pan, and pour boiling water upon it. Then make a lather as hot as the hands will bear. Take the flannel and wash it as quickly as possible. Done in this way flannel remains as soft as new, and is of a good colour.

Scotch method of washing flannels

Scrape one pound of soap, boil it down in sufficient water. When cooling beat it with the hand. It will be a sort of jelly. Add three tablespoonfuls of spirit of turpentine, and one of spirit of hartshorn. Wash the articles thoroughly in it, then rinse in cold water until all the soap is taken off, then in salt and water. Fold between two sheets, taking care not to allow two folds of the article washed to lie together. Mangle and iron with a very cool iron. Shawls, flannels, or other woollen articles done in this way look like new. Only use the salt where there are delicate colours that may strike.

To render boots and shoes waterproof

A good composition for winter use when it is desired to make boots proof against snow and wet, is composed of one part mutton suet and twice that quantity of beeswax, melted together. It should be applied to the leather at night, and the boot wiped with a flannel next morning. Although when the composition is first applied the leather will not polish as well as when blackened, yet will be susceptible of a brilliant polish after the blacking has been applied a few times.

The following composition not only renders the leather capable of resisting wet, but also makes it more pliable, softer and more durable. Dissolve half an ounce of Burgundy pitch in some drying oil, mixed with half an ounce of turpentine. To use this fluid, the boots should be made slightly warm by the fire and then painted over with the composition by means of a soft brush. Then allow them to dry and paint them over again with the liquid. The boots should then be placed in a warm and dry place until perfectly dry. Another composition of a similar kind is made by dissolving an ounce of powdered resin in a quarter of a pint of linseed-oil made hot over the fire in a pipkin. Then add two ounces of mutton suet from the kidney, chopped up small, and simmer until the materials are well mixed. This composition is applied like the last, but does not require a second application.

A French way of removing ink spots from linen

Melt a little fat, and dip the stained portion of the linen into it. When the article is washed the stains will disappear.

How to handle wet clothes

Handle a wet hat as lightly as possible. Wipe it as dry as you can with a clean handkerchief, and then brush it with a soft brush before you put it to dry. When nearly dry, go over it with a harder brush. If it still looks rough, damp it with a sponge dipped in vinegar or stale beer, and brush it with a hard brush till dry. When a coat gets wet wipe it down the way of the nap, with a sponge or silk handkerchief. Do not put wet boots or shoes near the fire.

Cleaning ostrich feathers

Put four ounces of white soap, cut small, dissolved in four pints of water, rather hot, in a large basin. Beat the solution into lather, introduce the feathers and rub well with the hands for five or six minutes. After the soaping, wash in clean water as hot as the hands can bear. Shake till dry.

To detect dampness in beds

First have the bed well warmed with a warming pan, then the moment the pan is taken out, introduce between the sheets an inverted glass tumbler. In a few minutes withdraw it. If the glass is covered with drops of wet or damp steam, the safest plan is to take off the sheets, and sleep between the blankets.

Laundry liquid and linens

Dissolve one quarter of a pound of lime in boiling water, strain it twice through a flannel bag. Dissolve separately half a pound of brown soap and half a pound of soda. Boil the three together. Put six gallons of water in a boiler, and, when boiling, add the mixture.

The linens, which must have been steeped in cold water for twelve hours, are wrung out, any stains rubbed with soap, and put into the boiler where they must boil for thirty five minutes. They are then drawn (the liquor being preserved, as it can be used three times), placed in a tub, and clear boiling water poured over them. Rub them out, rinse them well in cold water, and they are ready for drying. By this process two thirds of the ordinary labour of washing is saved; bleaching is dispensed with entirely; the clothes are much clearer, and are less worn than by the ordinary mode of washing, and the mixture in no way damages the fabric. Ere long, that fruitful source of annoyance and discomfort, 'the washing day,' will, by the use of this mixture, come we are assured, to be reckoned among the things that were.

Cleaning straw matting

Matting may be cleaned with a large coarse cloth, dipped in salt and water, and then wiped dry. The salt prevents the straw from turning yellow.

An easy way to clean silver articles

Set fire to some wheat-straw, collect the ashes, and after powdering it, sift it through muslin. Polish the silver plate with a little of it applied to some soft leather.

Steel forks

Steel forks are readily cleaned by having a pot of damp moss or hay, with some sand intermixed, into which they may be repeatedly thrust. If knives or forks get an unpleasant taint which cannot be removed readily, they may be plunged into the mould of the garden, which has a very absorptive power, arid rapidly removes such odours.

To clean a kettle

A flat oyster shell put into a tea kettle and kept constantly there will prevent the formation of crust upon the inside, by attracting the stony particles that are in the water to itself.

To clean marble

Take two parts of common soda, one part of pumice stone, and one part of finely powdered chalk. Sift it rough a fine sieve and mix it with water. Rub it well all over the marble, and the stains will be removed. Then wash the marble over with soap and water, and it will be clean as it was at first.

Mock alabaster

To make plaster of Paris look like alabaster, dip them in a pail containing a strong solution of alum and water.

Cleaning Japanned goods

Japanned goods such as tea trays, should not have boiling water poured upon them, but should be washed with warm water, and polished with a piece of wash leather and fine flour.

To preserve pencil marks

Dip the paper upon which you have the drawing or writing into a dish of skimmed milk. Then dry it, and iron it on the wrong side. In ironing paper do not let the iron rest a moment, as it will leave a crease or mark, but go over it at rapidly as possible.

Washing paint

The best mode to wash paint is to take some fine bath brick, and when you have nibbed some soap on the flannel dip it in the brick. This will remove the grease and dirt speedily, without injury.

Rice flour cement

An excellent cement may be made from flour by mixing the flour with water; gently simmer over the fire.

Egg and lime cement

The white of an egg well beaten with quick lime and a small quantity of very old cheese is an excellent cement for china, glass, etc.

Liquid glue

Take a wide-mouthed bottle and dissolve in it eight ounces of best glue in half-a-pint of water by setting it in a vessel of water and heating until dissolved, then add slowly two-and-a-half ounces of strong aquafortis (nitric acid), stirring all the while. Keep it well corked, and it will be ready for use at any moment.

Crickets

To destroy crickets, put snuff into the holes and cracks from whence they come out.

Sheepskins for home use

The following particulars will be found useful to those who desire to prepare sheepskins for home use. First of all, wash the wool in strong soap suds, the water being just warm enough to feel comfortable to the hand. It will be necessary to pick out the loose dirt from the wool; then scrub and rub the skin on a board. A tablespoonful of kerosene added to three gallons of warm suds will greatly help the cleansing process. Change the water until the wool looks white and clean. Then put the skin into cold water enough to cover it, and dissolve half a pound of salt and the same quantity of alum in about three pints of boiling water; pour the mixture over the skin; rinse it up and down, then let it soak twelve hours; after that hang it over a fence or a line to drain.

When well drained stretch it on a board to dry, or nail it on the wall, wool side towards the boards. When nearly dry, rub into the skins one ounce of powdered alum and saltpetre (if the skin is large, double the quantity); rub this in for an hour or so. To do this readily, the skin must be taken down and spread on a table or flat surface. Fold the skins in sides, together, and hang it away. Rub it every day for three days, or till perfect. Scrape off the skin with a stick or a blunt knife till cleared of all loose skin or bits of flesh or dirt; then rub it with pumice stone, or rotten stone will do. Trim it to a good shape, and you have an excellent skin for any purpose. Any intelligent housewife can dye it green, blue, or scarlet with the so called "family dyes," either in powder or liquid.

To destroy black beetles

A certain remedy is to procure some bracken, or common fern. Put it down about the house at night. The black beetles will eat it ravenously and soon die, and their relatives will pick their bones. It is commonly used in the north of England.

To soften old putty

In removing old broken panes of glass from windows, it is often very difficult to get off the hard, dry putty that sticks round the glass and its frame. Dip a small brush into a little nitric or muriatic acid, and go over the putty with it. Let it rest awhile, and it will become so soft that you can remove it with ease.

Varnish for paper hangings, maps, prints etc

Take of genuine pale Canadian balsam and rectified oil of turpentine in equal parts, and mix thoroughly. Give the articles two coats of size before varnishing.

Substitutes & modern terms

Whether used in cooking or around the home, some of these ingredients are easily substituted with modern equivalents. Some caution needs to be taken with the household items and you should follow directions carefully.

Anchovy essence	Made from pulped anchovies. A suitable substitute is fish sauce or Worstershire sauce
Brown soap	Natural soap usually glycerine based
Burgundy pitch	Resin usually derived from the Spruce pine tree
Canadian balsam	Resin usually derived from the Balsam fir tree
Capon	A cockerel or neutered rooster
Citron	A variety of lemon usually with a thicker rind and little juice
Clarified butter	The pure fat of butter when it is separated from its solids. Has a higher burning point and a more intense flavour. A suitable substitute is ghee.
Comfits	Candied dried fruit
Corn starch	Derived from maize or corn but in Australia is typically made from wheat. When used as a thickener, cornflour is usually used.
Dutch oven	A heavy earthenware or iron pot with a close fitting lid
Faggot of herbs	See sweet herbs
Flannel jelly bag	Made from unbleached calico or muslin large enough to tie a knot
Fricassee	Diced meats that have been sautéed or braised

Ground rice	Made from rice, it is typically used as a thickener. It is coarser than rice flour
Indian meal	Ground corn or maize
Indian pickle	Spicy or sweet relish or chutney
Isinglass	Derived from fish bladders, todays substitute is gelatine
Jamaica pepper	Commonly called allspice
Ketchup or catsup	Usually made into a sauce using tomatoes and spices
Laurel leaf	Bay leaf
Loaf, pounded or lump sugar	Regular sugar that has been formed into a loaf. In colonial times, sugar was usually sold in loaves rather than in its granulated free flowing form we know today.
Mace	Part of the nutmeg seed, it imparts a more pepper flavour than the more commonly used kernel of actual nutmeg, however, regular nutmeg may be used as a substitute.
Moist sugar	Today commonly referred to as brown sugar or muscovado sugar
Mushroom catsup	Non-tomato form of ketchup made from mushrooms and spices. A suitable substitute is soy sauce or Worstershire sauce
Mushroom powder	Dried and ground mushrooms. Used when a mushroom flavour is required but not the texture.
Neatsfoot oil	Made from leg bones of cattle to retain an oil form
Nitrate of potash, nitrate of soda	See saltpetre
Orange flower water	Made from distilled orange blossoms or a tea infused with orange blossoms
Penny loaf	Yeast free soda bread
Penny royal	A flowering herb imparting a spearmint flavour
Pimento	Sweet pepper. When used in powdered form, a suitable substitute is allspice

Powdered resin	Used in glue making, its powdered form is often available in craft stores
Quick lime	Used as a binding agent in some cement compounds.
Ratafia	Fortified wine
Red sage	A herb common in Chinese medicine
Sack	Dry white wine
Saltpetre	A very volatile chemical used in everything from explosives to fertiliser. In old times, was often used to cure meats. Caution is advised.
Scald	In cooking today, commonly referred to a simmering or blanching
Scrag of mutton	Usually the most inexpensive part of the meat. Lamb neck would be today's substitute.
Seville oranges	Rough skinned in appearance and quite bitter or tart to taste when eaten as a fruit. Often used in production of marmalade.
Shell lime	Made from burned and crushed shells such as oyster shells, used as a binding agent in some cement compounds.
Snuff	Ground or powdered dried tobacco leaves
Spirit of hartshorn	Made from deer antler, todays substitute is household ammonia
Sweet herbs	Usually a bunch of herbs tied together, now more commonly described as a bouquet garni
Tartaric acid	Cream of tartar
Unsmoked bacon	Pork that has been cured without smoking, todays substitute is pancetta.
Verjuice	Made from pressed unripened grapes, often used as a substitute for vinegar
Volatile salts	Smelling salts, see spirit of hartshorn
Walnut liquor	Made from pressed unripened walnuts

White beet	A sweeter version of the traditional red beetroot
White gravy	A white sauce made with flour, milk, salt and pepper
White stock	Stock made from blanched or boiled bones rather than roast bones

Measures & conversions

Oven guides

Colonial cooking temperatures depended not only the size and shape of the oven but also the fuel used, especially when the appliance merely meant a pot strung over a campfire. The following table should provide a rough guide for the modern cook.

	Celsius	Fahrenheit
Cool oven	90°c	200°f
Very slow oven	120°c	250°f
Slow oven or slack fire	150–160°c	300–325°f
Moderately slow	160–180°c	325–350°f
Moderate oven	180–190°c	350–375°f
Moderately hot or sharp fire	190–200°c	375–400°f
Hot or quick oven	200–230°c	400–450°f
Very hot oven	230–260°c	450–500°f
Fast or fierce oven	230–260°c	450–500°f

Weights & measures

One gallon	4550ml or 4.5 litres
One gill	142ml or 0.15 litres
One ounce	28gm or 28ml
One pint	570ml or 0.6 litres
One quart	1140ml or 1.14 litres

Index

Meats   5

Beef a la mode	12
Beef rump en Matelotte	5
Beef steaks and oyster sauce	6
Beefsteak and oyster pie	7
Boiling a ham	8
Bubble and squeak	12
Calf's brains a la maître d'hôtel	14
Chartreuse	9
China chils	8
Chine of pork, roasted	15
Cold beef pudding	9
Concentrated beef	16
Dutch fricandel	15
Fried veal and oyster patties	13
Hashed mutton	14
Indian burdman stew	11
Italian beef steaks	11
Juicy corned beef	13
Lamb cutlets with spinach	6
Leftover roast beef pudding	14
Marrow bones	9
Meat and potato pie	5
Meat cakes	10
Meat patties	8
Minced collops	7
Mutton scallops	5
Pilau	6
Roast lamb quarter	13
Roast pork leg	10
Roast tripe	15
Scotch hotch potch	10
Sheep's kidneys	10
Sheep's tongues in paper	15
Staffordshire beef steaks	9
Steak or kidney pudding	6
Trotters a la poulette	13

Poultry   17

Boiled duck	20
Chicken curry	20
Chicken or fowl salad	20
Chicken rissoles	19
Cock-a-leekie	17
Duck hash	19
Giblet pie	17
Roasted duck	18
Stewed chicken with wine	18
Stewed fowl and rice	18

Seafood — 21

Baked pike with oyster	24
Cod pie	23
Collared salmon	24
Crayfish	23
Eel pie	22
Lobster or crab cutlets	22
Minced crab	24
Oyster and sweetbread pie	22
Oyster fritters	23
Persian kedgeree	24
Potato and fish cakes	22
Salmon with white sauce	21
Trumpeter whiting	21

Game — 25

Emu	25
Fricasseed rabbit	29
Hare soup	28
Hare	28
Hashed venison or kangaroo	27
Kangaroo steamer	27
Rabbit pie	29
Roast kangaroo	25
Roman pie	29
Slippery bob	28
Stewed pigeon	25
Sticker up spitted kangaroo	26
Wild duck	28

Soups & stews — 31

Clam soup	32
Cock a leekie soup	36
Forcemeat for mock turtle	34
Giblet soup	31
Hare soup	37
Irish stew	37
Macaroni soup	31
Mutton mock turtle	33
Ox tail soup	38
Palestine soup	39
Pea soup	38
Pumpkin soup	36
Small eggs for mock turtle	33
Soup kitchen soup	39
Soup maigre	33
Veal mock turtle	35
Vegetable soup	38

Vegetables & accompaniments — 41

Baked German cauliflower	50
Baked tomatoes	47
Balloon Potatoes	49
Boiled parsnips	50
Cayenne cheese biscuits	46
Cheese pudding	46
Cole cannon	44
Cracknels	44
Crisp parsley	45
Egg toast	51
Fricassee of parsnips	43
Macaroni	46
New potatoes	41
Norfolk dumplings	43
Onions stuffed	49
Panada	43
Peas pudding	42
Pickled nasturtiums	41
Pickled tomatoes	49

Pork jelly	51
Potato chips	46
Potato pastey	42
Potato wall	41
Preserved cucumbers	44
Preserved green peas	48
Preserved tomatoes	47
Puff pastry	52
Stewed celery	44
Stewed cucumbers	42
Stewed tomatoes	46
Surprise eggs for parties	51
Tomato pie	49
Tomato salad	45
Vegetable quarter	42

Sauces 53

Beef brose	54
Beef stock	58
Bread sauce	55
Dutch sauce	56
Egg sauce	56
Fish sauce a la craster	54
Gravy without any meat	57
Hams or tongues glazing	56
Lobster sauce	56
Oyster sauce	57
Sage cream	53
Sauce a la tartare	53
Sauce for boiled fish	57
Sauce for rabbits	55
Sauce for wild fowl	54
Sauce piquante	53
Sauce poivrade	54
Sauce Robert	53
Sharp sauce for venison, hare or kangaroo	53

Tomato ketchup	57
White sauce	58
Wine sauce	56

Cakes, biscuits & breads 59

Almond icing	69
Amber Pudding	63
Apple butter	66
Bread and butter pudding	59
Bread	61
Breakfast rolls	64
Common teacake	63
Corn bread	63
Cream meringues	70
Damper	64
German pancake	68
Ginger bread nuts	66
Gingerbread cake	70
Gingerbread	64
Gingerbread	72
Light sponge cake	72
Liquid Balm or Yeast	60
Mince pies	65
Norfolk biscuits	69
Orange tart	67
Plain cake	68
Portugal cakes	67
Preserved bread	64
Puff paste (pastry) with brandy	71
Rich cherry and almond cake	70
Rook cakes	59
Rose water and orange biscuits	67
Shortbread	59
Small plum cakes	68
Sultana cake	67

Sweet potato fritters	63
Tea biscuit	68
Victoria sandwiches	72
Water cakes	68

Puddings & pancakes   73

Apple cheese	86
Apple puffs	83
Apple snow	79
Arrowroot pudding	80
Baked cheesecake	78
Baked tapioca pudding	81
Biscuit pudding	83
Brown bread pudding	86
Chocolate pie	82
Christmas plum pudding	76
Coconut pudding	82
Coffee ice pudding	87
Cream pancakes	79
Curd fritters	84
Dutch curd pudding	75
Eve's pudding	80
Excellent potato pudding	77
German puddings or puffs	81
Ground rice pudding	77
Iced hamburgh pudding	73
Irish pancakes	80
Light paste (pastry) for tarts and cheesecakes	73
Marrow pudding	86
Minute pudding	82
Muscatel plum pudding	77
Oatmeal pudding	84
Orange pudding	74
Pink fritters	84

Potato balls	74
Potato fritters	74
Potato fritters	85
Prune tart	73
Quaking pudding	77
Quick pudding	75
Raised doughnuts	82
Rice pancakes	80
Royal fritters	85
Shelford pudding	85
Small potato cheesecakes	78
Soufflé pudding	74
Spanish fritters	84
Sponge pudding	86
Suet pudding	87

Jams, jellies & sherbets   89

Apple jelly	90
Black cherry preserve	89
Black currant sherbet	91
Blackberry jam	93
Bottled raspberry preserve	92
Cherry jam	93
Cherry sherbet	92
Currant and raspberry sherbet	91
Damson jelly	89
Jelly for cakes	91
Melon jam	89
Plum preserve	91
Quince jelly	90
Rhubarb preserve	93
Strawberry and raspberry acid	90

Custards & sauces 95

Almond custard	95
American butter sauce	97
Devonshire butter	98
Glazing for tarts	97
Lemon cream	95
Ornamented custard pudding	96
Rice blacmange	97
Seville orange custard	96
Spanish sherbet	95
Thick vanilla cream	96
Vanilla cream	98
Wine or brandy sauce	96

Drinks 99

Apple cider	102
Barley water	99
Bitter Ale	100
Crambambuli punch	99
Currant water	99
Ginger beer	100
King cup	100
Lemon sherbet	101
Orangeade	101
Punch a la romaine	99
Raisin wine	102
Rhubarb wine	102
Veal sherbet	101

Around the home 103

A French way of removing ink spots from linen	108
A useful lotion	105
An easy way to clean silver articles	110
Antidote for poison ivy, insect bites	104
Chest colds	103
Cleaning Japanned goods	110
Cleaning ostrich feathers	108
Cleaning straw matting	110
Common cough	103
Crickets	111
Cure for corns	104
Egg and lime cement	111
For hoarseness	103
Hair wash	105
Homemade soap	104
How to handle wet clothes	108
Keeping flowers	105
Laundry liquid and linens	109
Liquid glue	111
Mock alabaster	110
Mustard whey	104
Relief for asthma	104
Rice flour cement	111
Scotch method of washing flannels	106
Sheepskins for home use	112
Steel forks	110
To clean a kettle	110
To clean marble	110
To destroy black beetles	113
To detect dampness in beds	108
To preserve geraniums during winter	106
To preserve pencil marks	111
To render boots and shoes waterproof	107
To renovate black silk	105
To soften old putty	113
To wash flannels	106

Toilet vinegar	103
Toothache	103
Varnish for paper hangings, maps, prints etc	113
Washing paint	111
Waterproof for leather boots	106